T0072031

BROOKLYN BOUND

A COLORING BOOK

INCLUDING
WILLIAMSBURG
PROSPECT PARK
CONEY ISLAND
AND MORE

ILLUSTRATED BY
MIKAYLA SHERFY

ULYSSES PRESS

Illustrations copyright © 2023 Mikayla Sherfy. Concept and design copyright © 2023 Ulysses Press and its licensors. All rights reserved. Any unauthorized duplication in whole or in part or dissemination of this edition by any means (including but not limited to photocopying, electronic devices, digital versions, and the internet) will be prosecuted to the fullest extent of the law.

Published by:
Ulysses Press
PO Box 3440
Berkeley, CA 94703
www.ulyssespress.com

ISBN: 978-1-64604-509-9

Printed in the United States
10 9 8 7 6 5 4 3 2

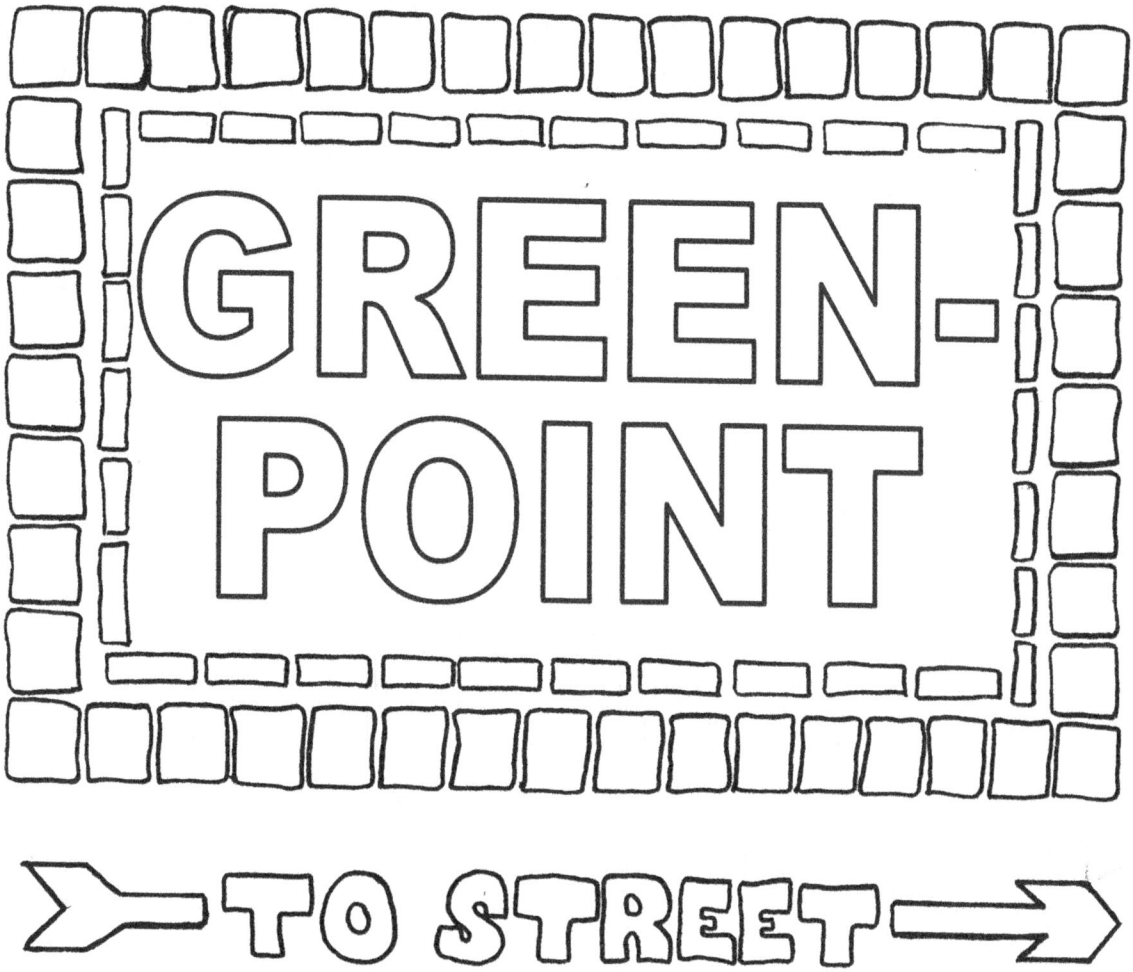
GREEN-
POINT
TO STREET

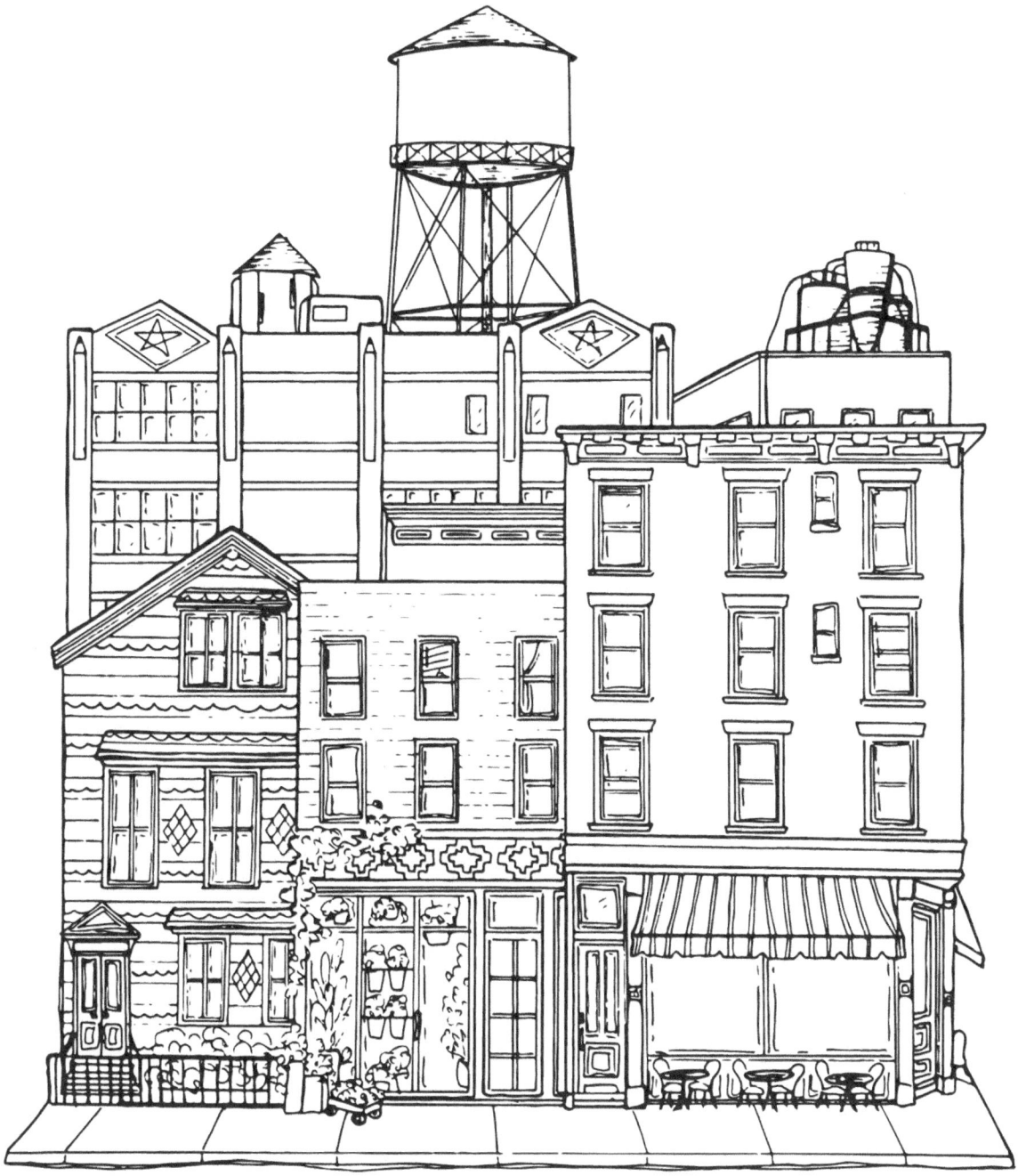

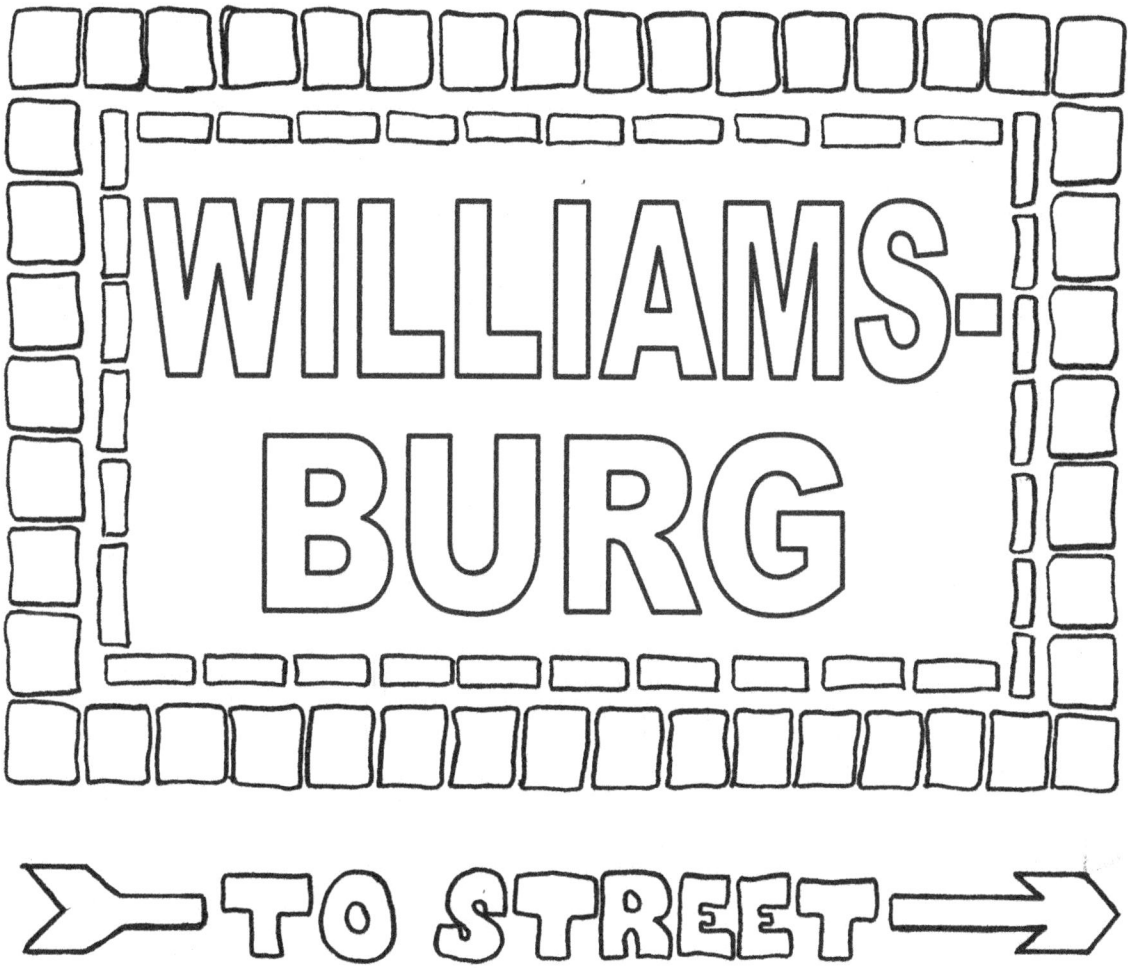
WILLIAMS-
BURG
TO STREET

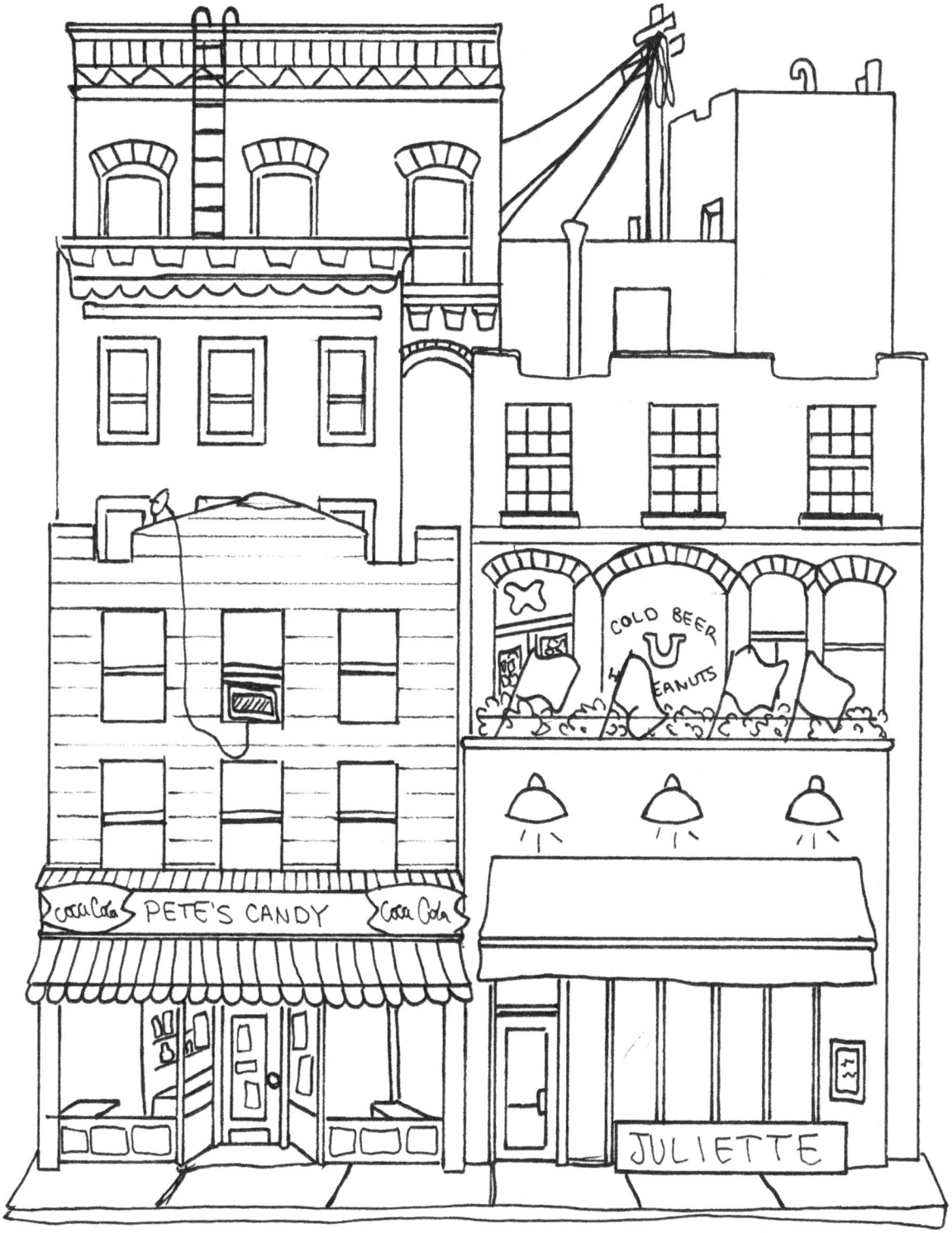
COLD BEER
PEANUTS
Coca Cola
PETE'S CANDY
Coca Cola
JULIETTE

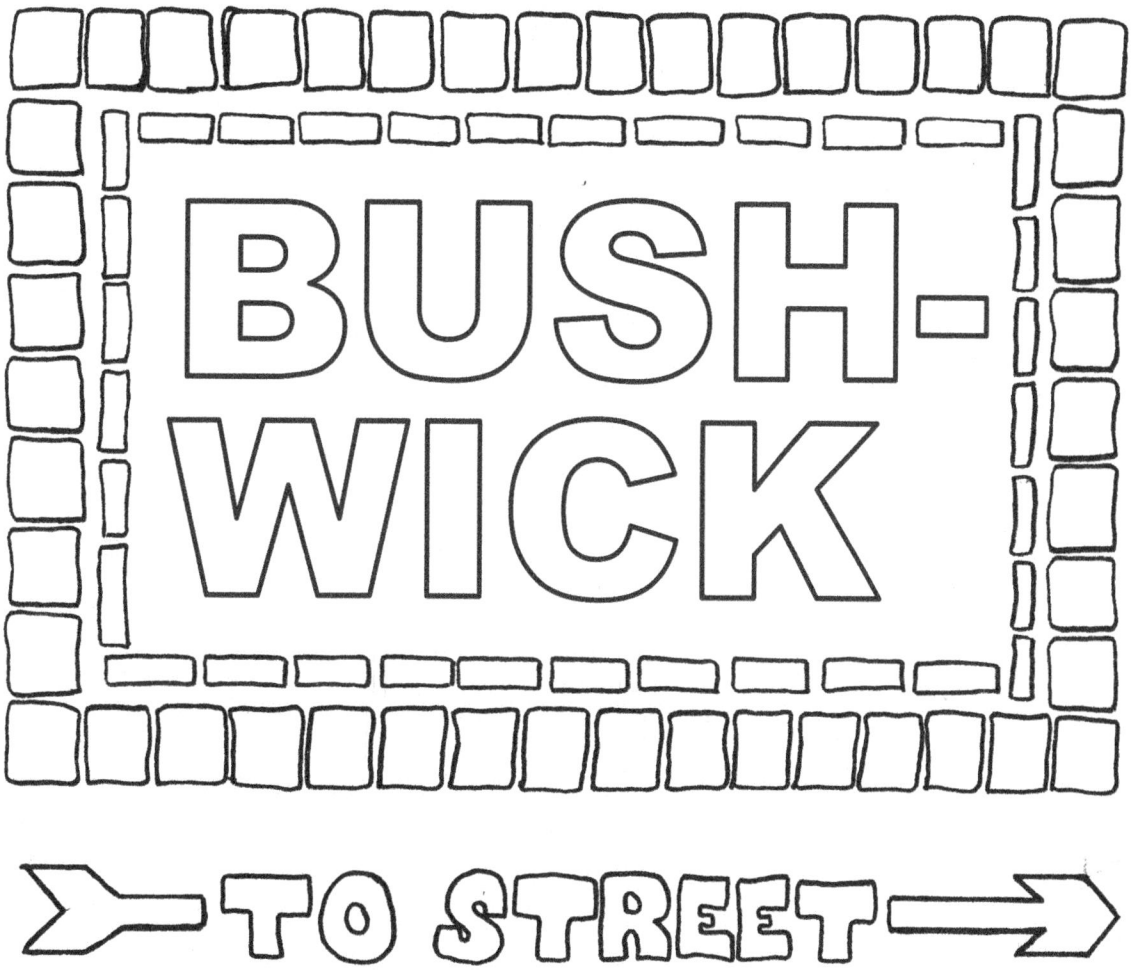
BUSH-
WICK
TO STREET

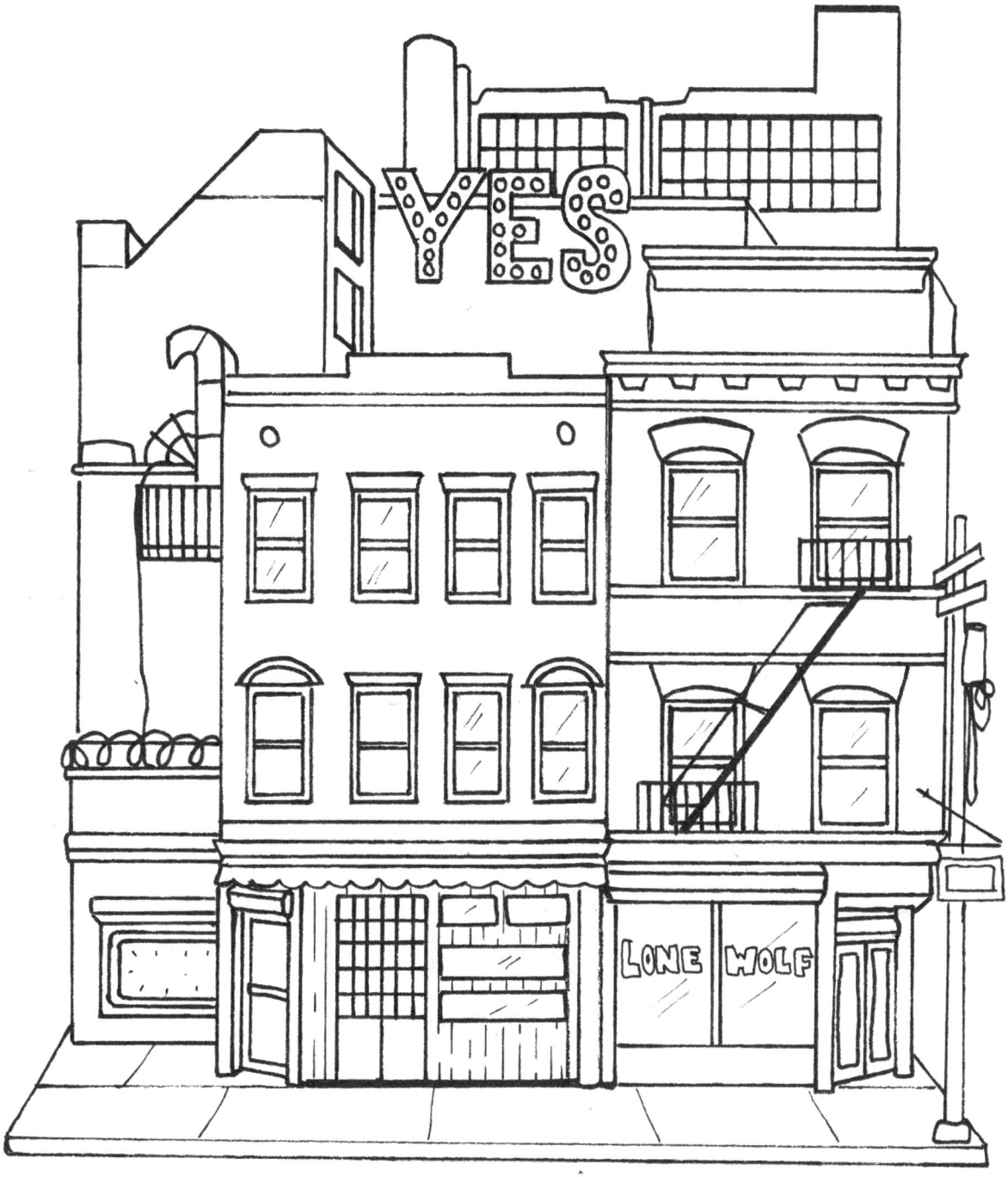
YES
LONE WOLF

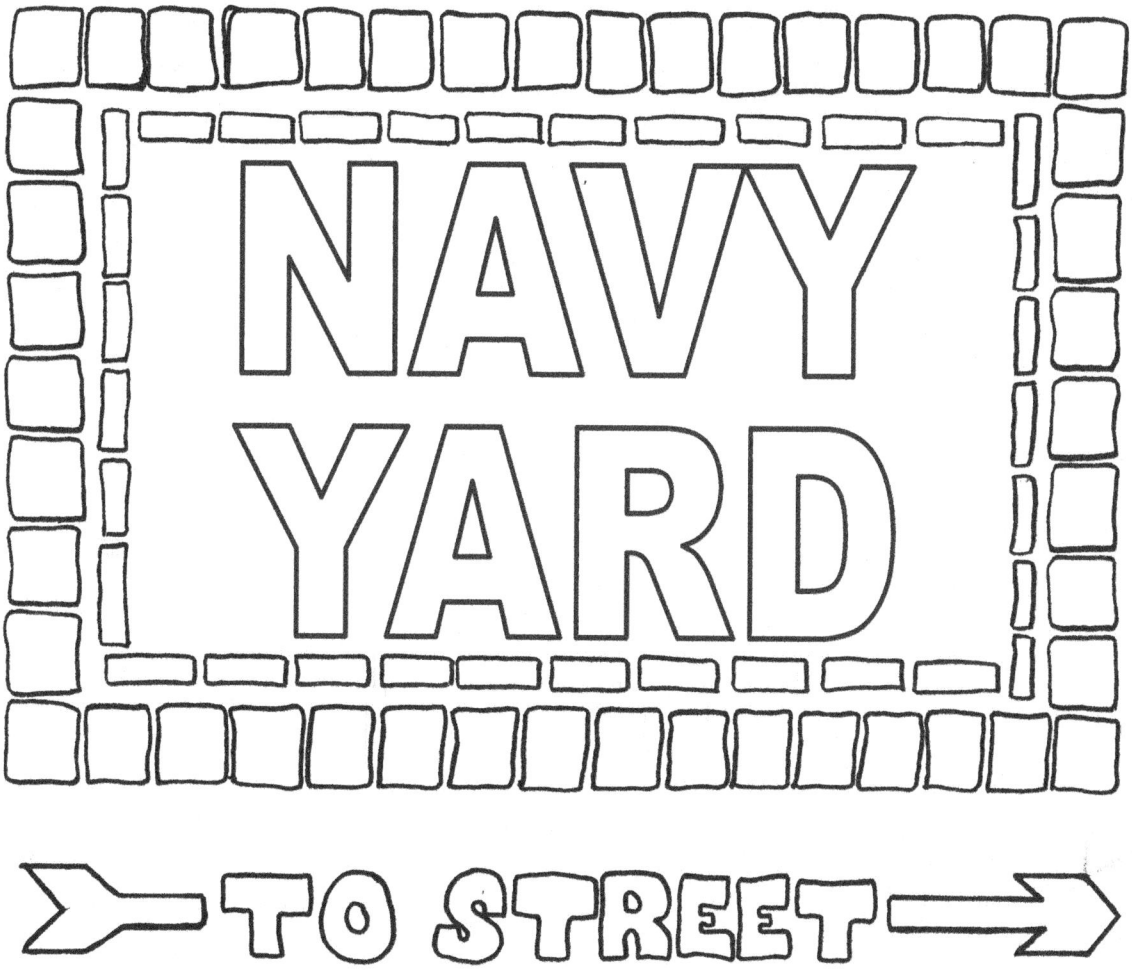
NAVY
YARD
TO STREET

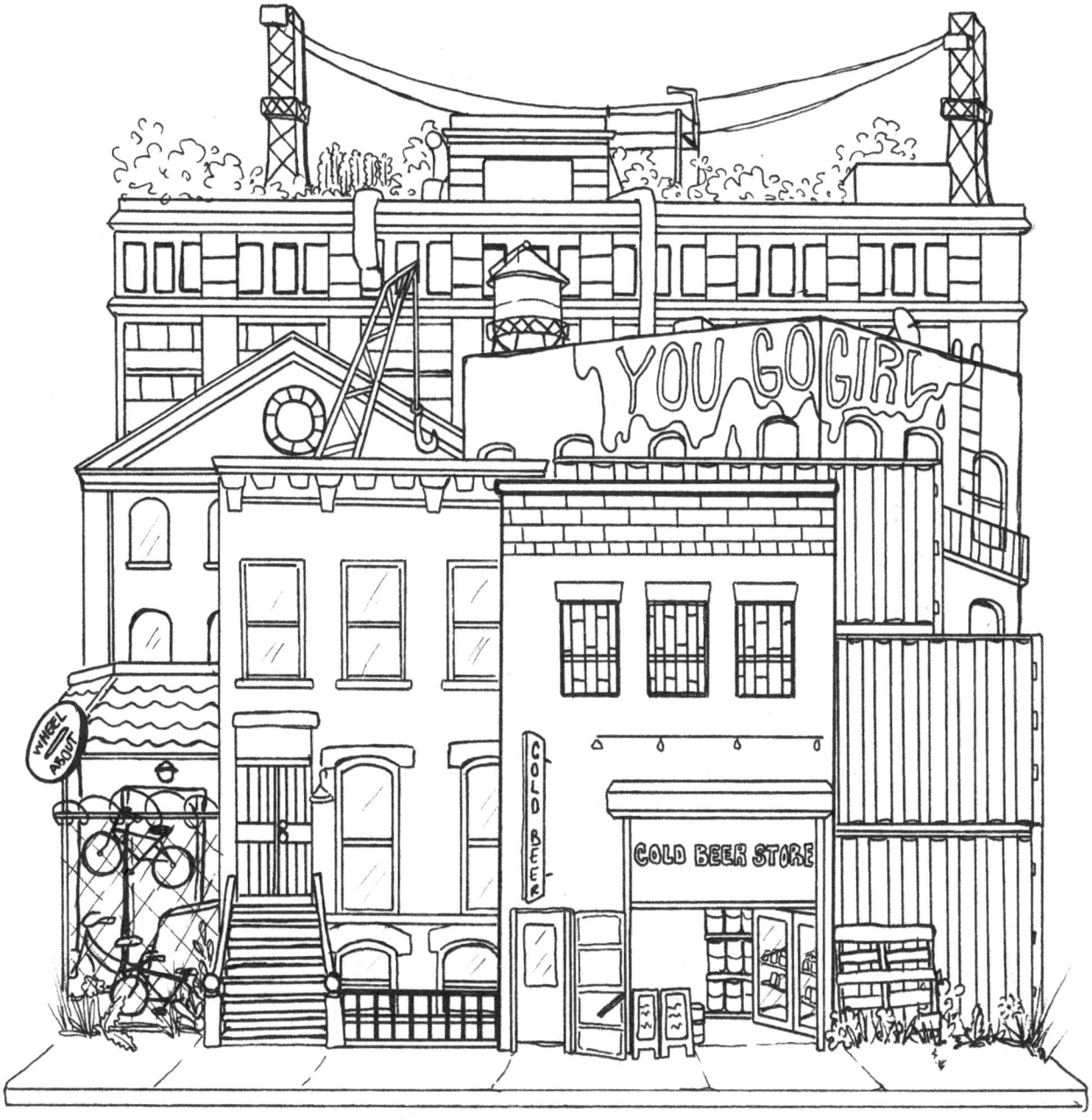
YOU GO GIRL
WHEEL AROUND
COLD BEER
COLD BEER STORE

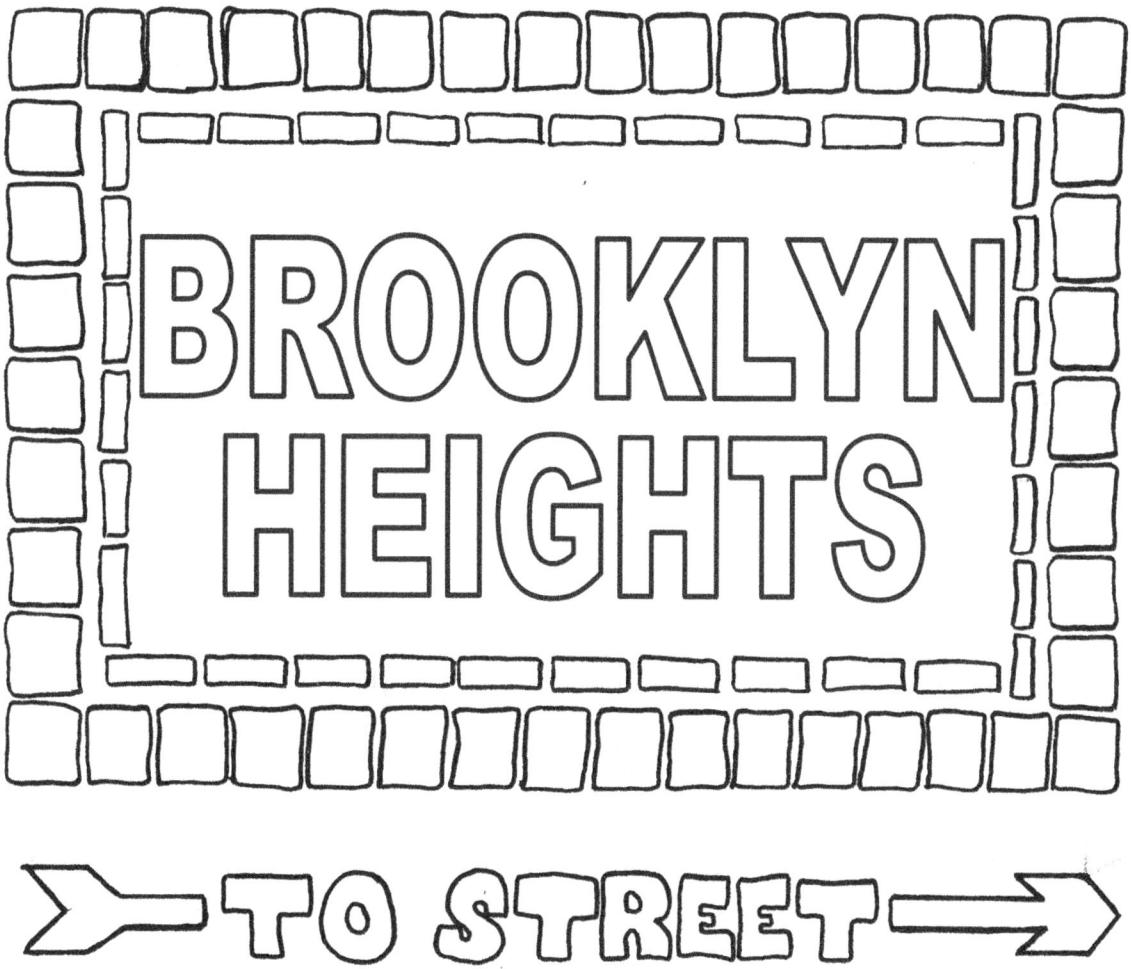
BROOKLYN
HEIGHTS
TO STREET

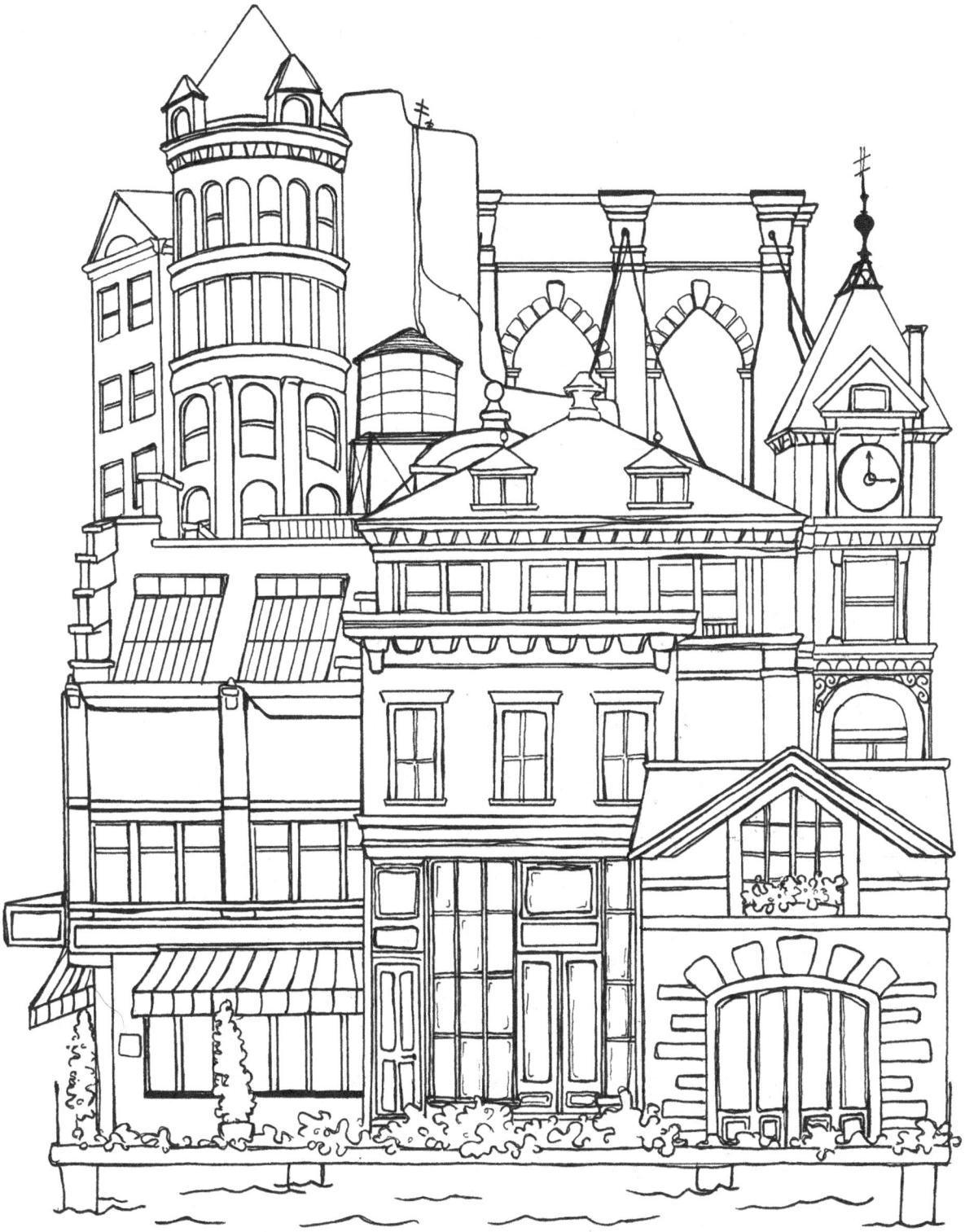

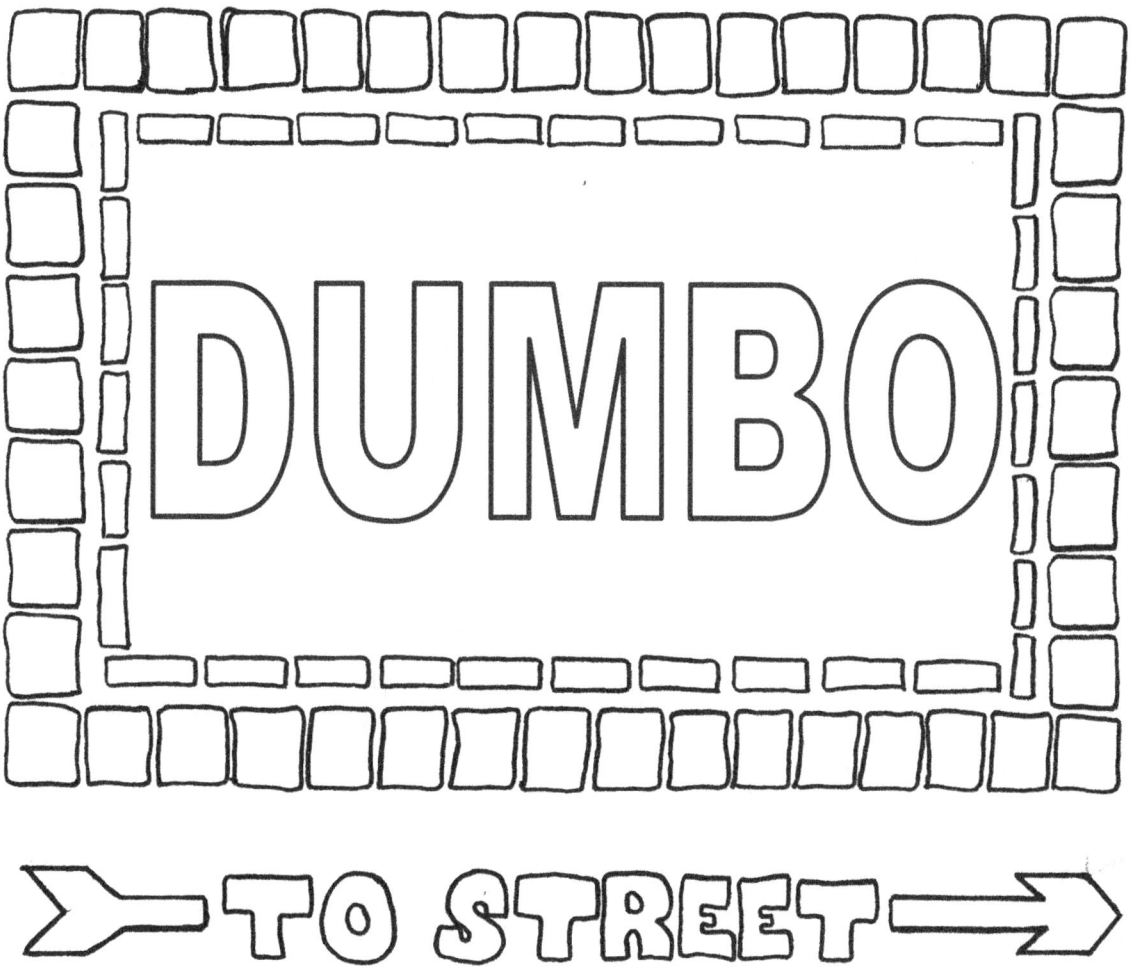
DUMBO
TO STREET

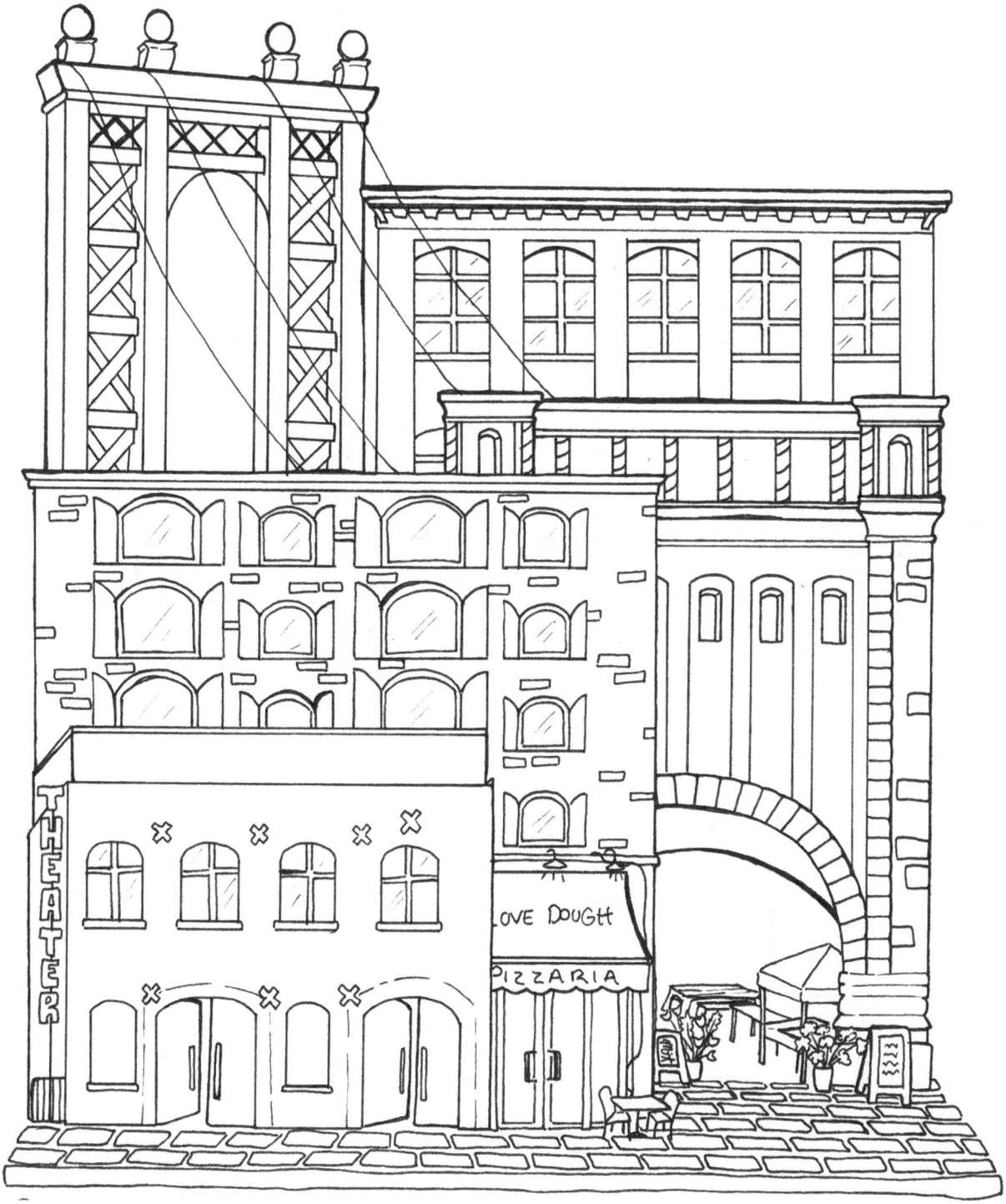
THEATER
LOVE DOUGH
PIZZARIA

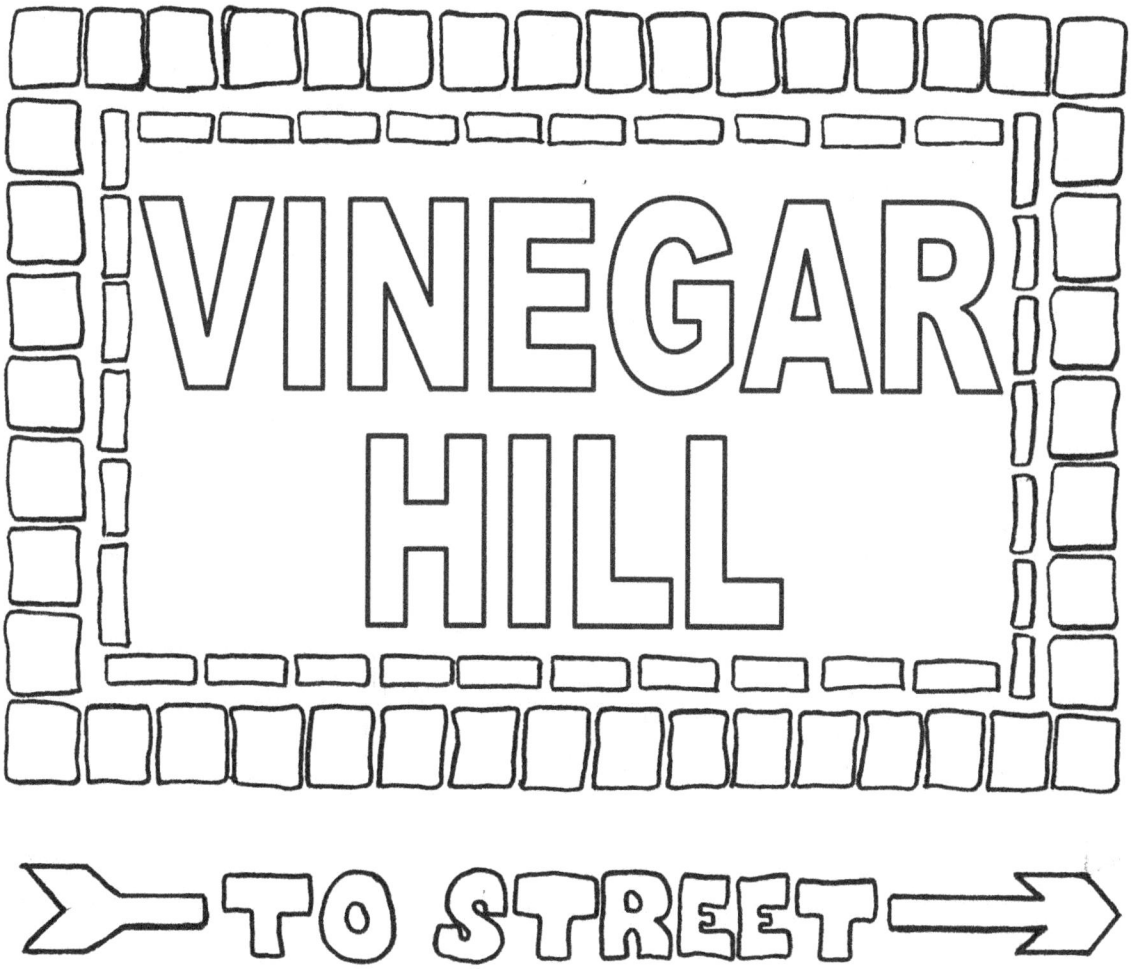
VINEGAR
HILL
TO STREET

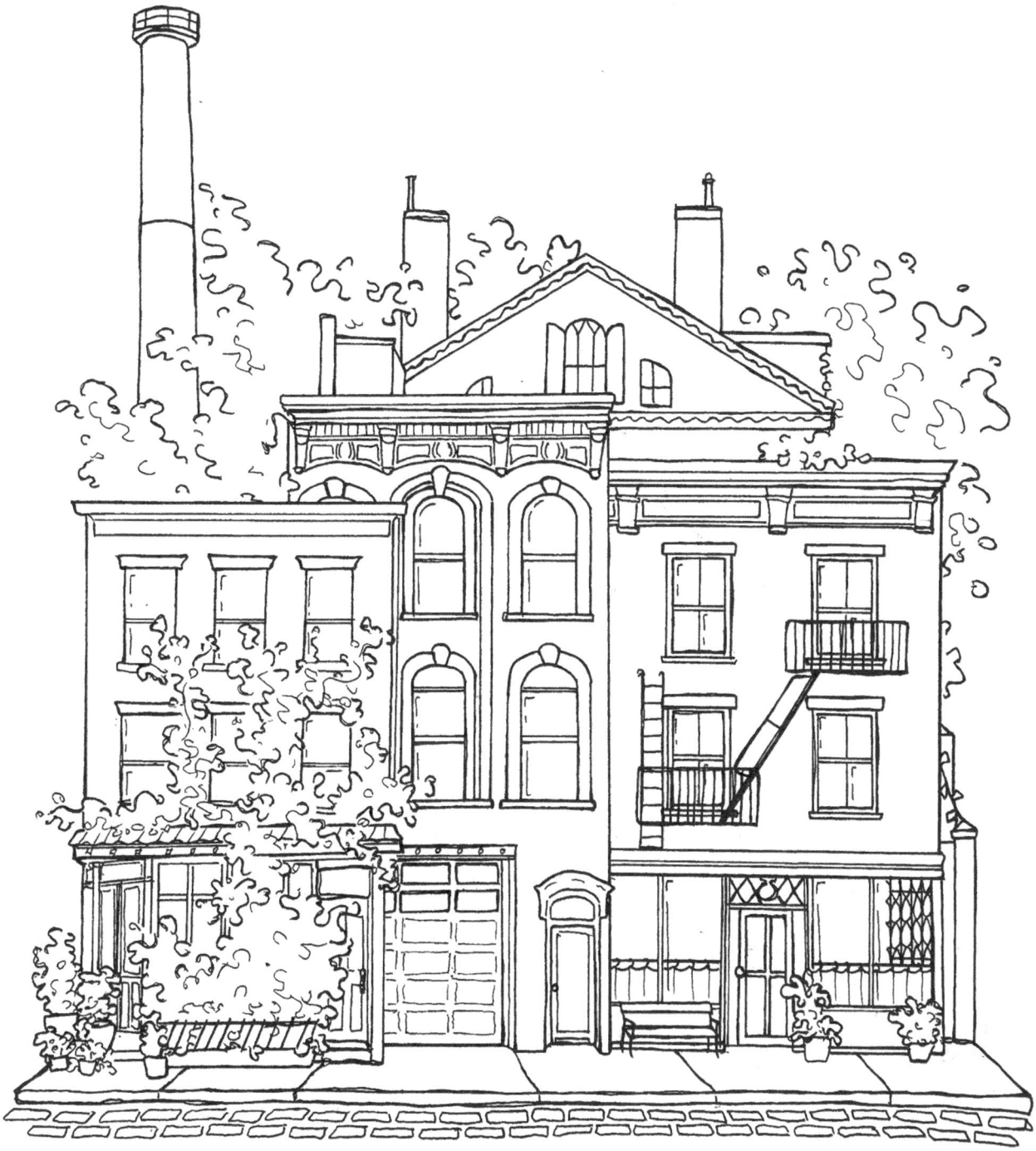

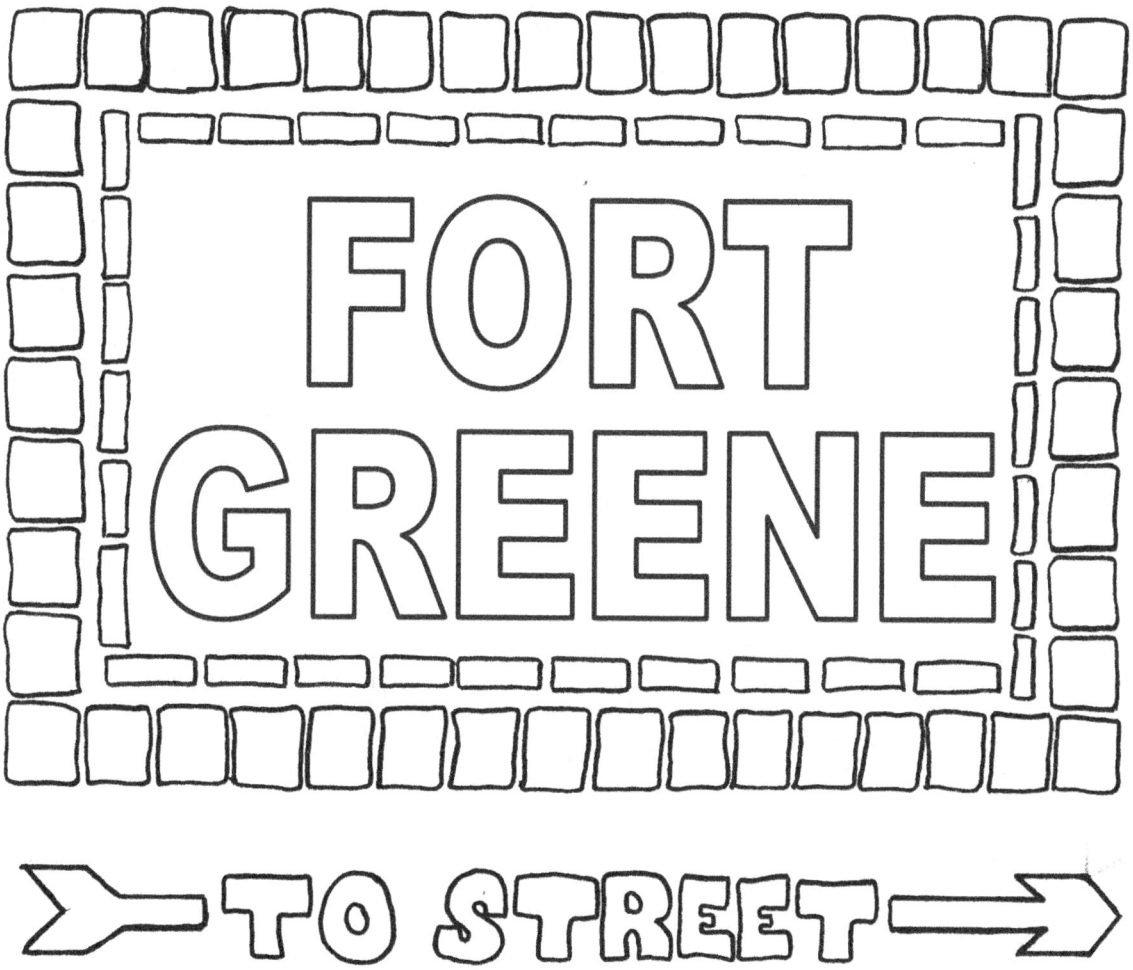
FORT
GREENE
TO STREET

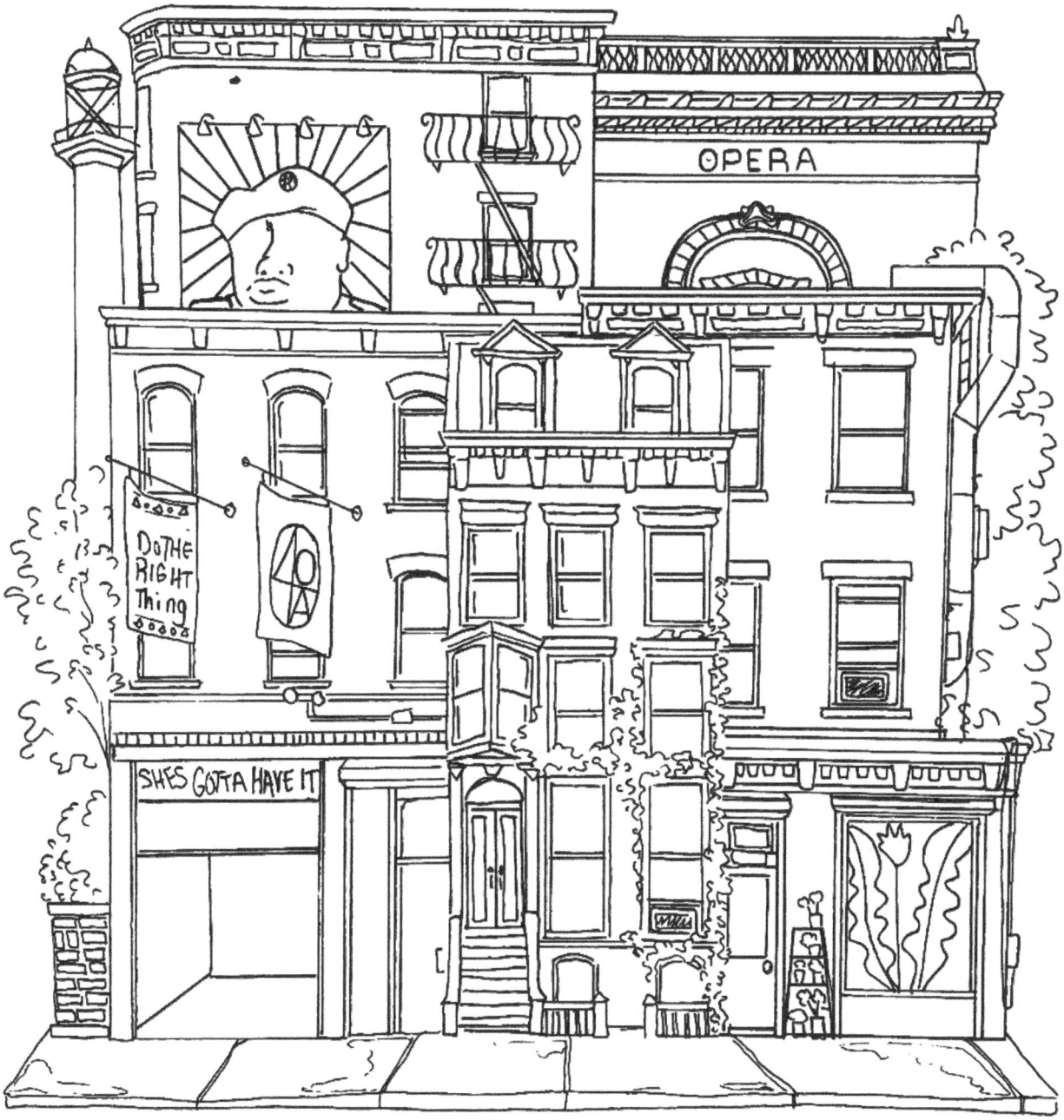
OPERA
DO THE RIGHT Thing
SHES GOTTA HAVE IT

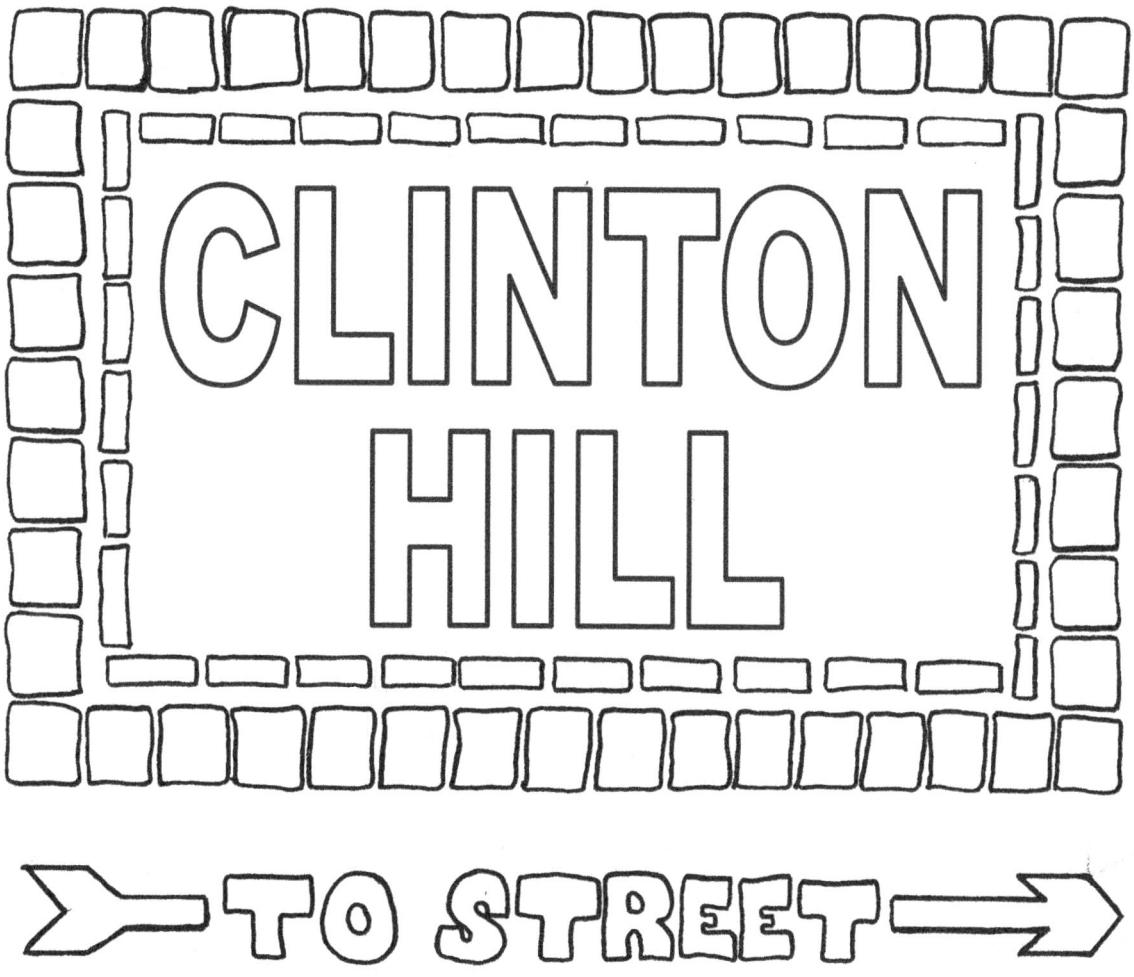
CLINTON
HILL
TO STREET

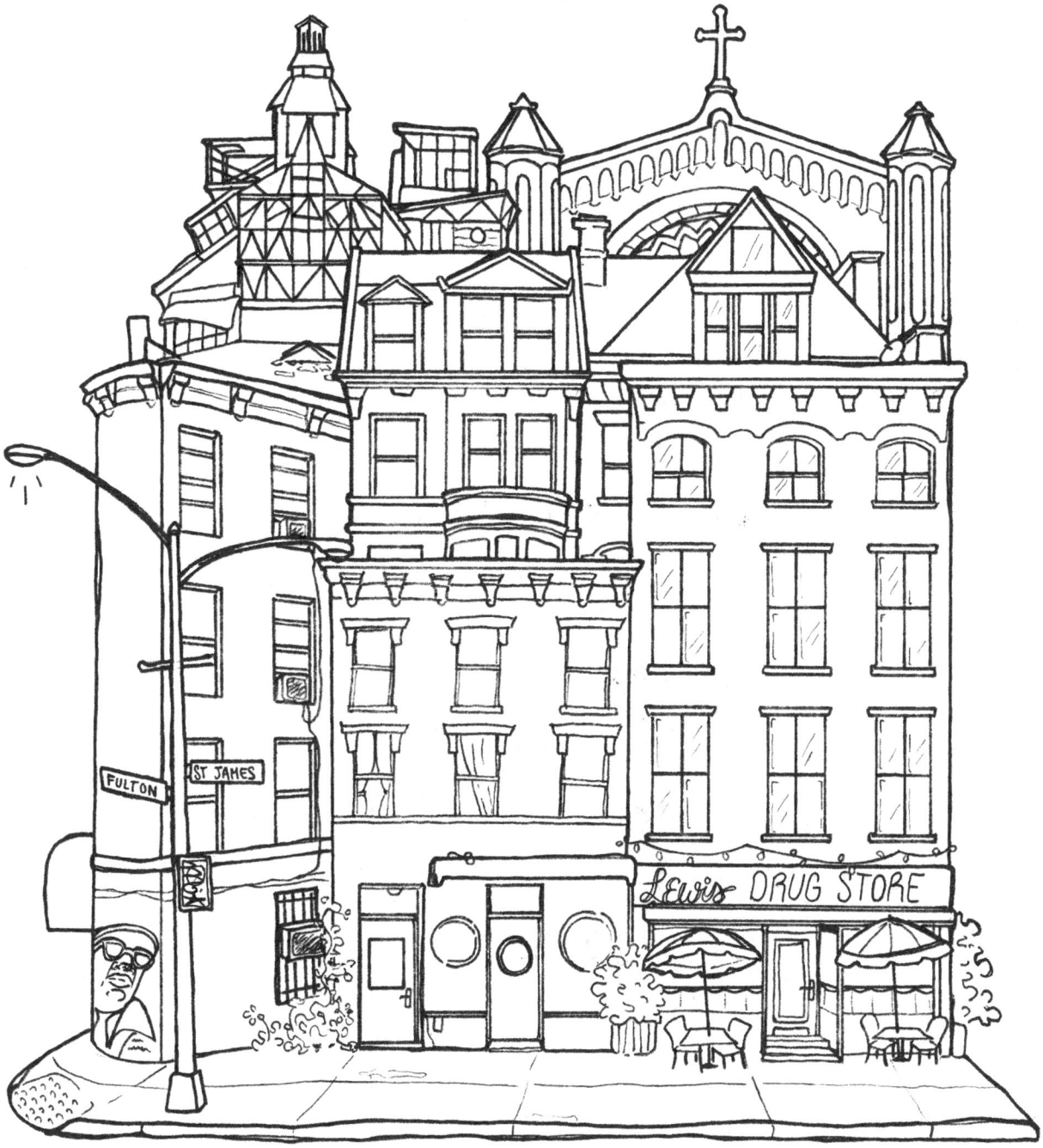
FULTON
ST JAMES
Lewis DRUG STORE

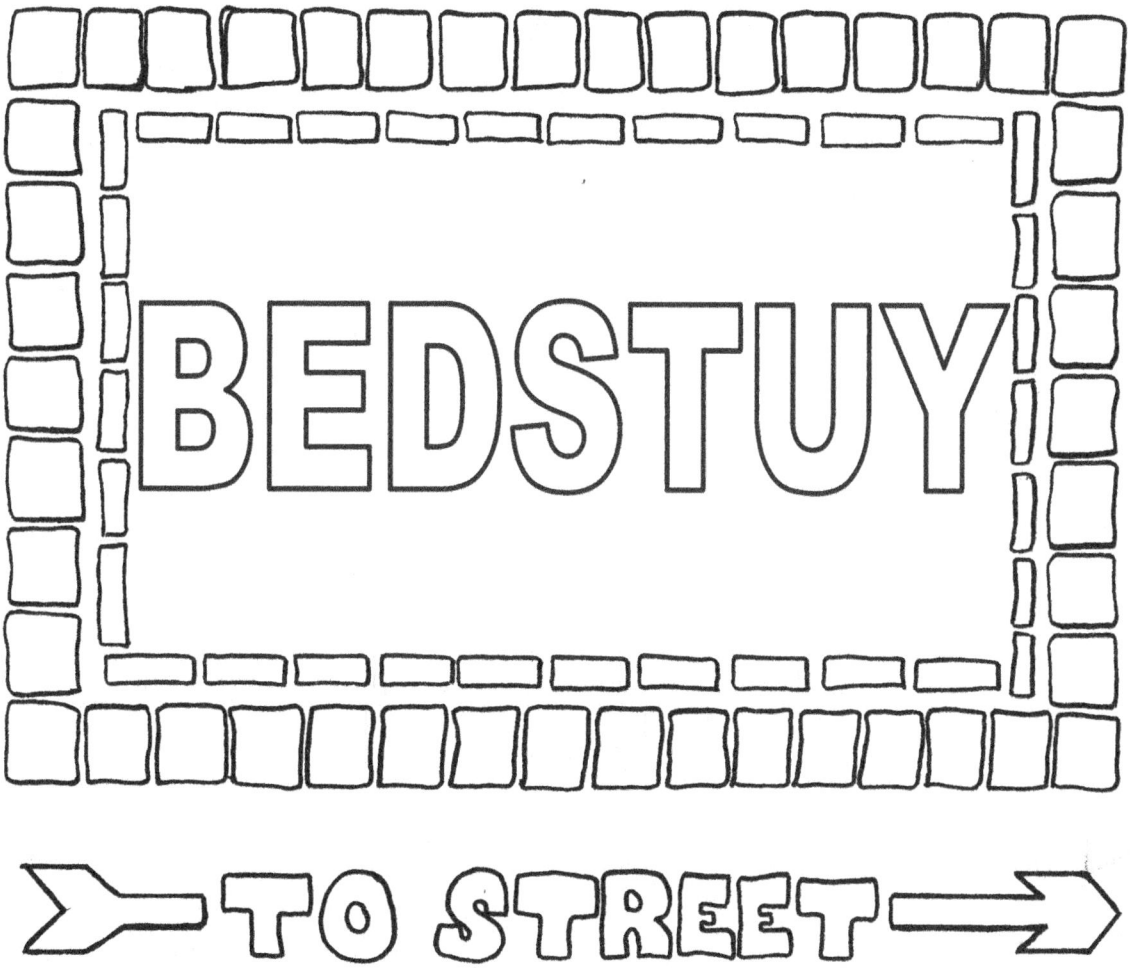
BEDSTUY
TO STREET

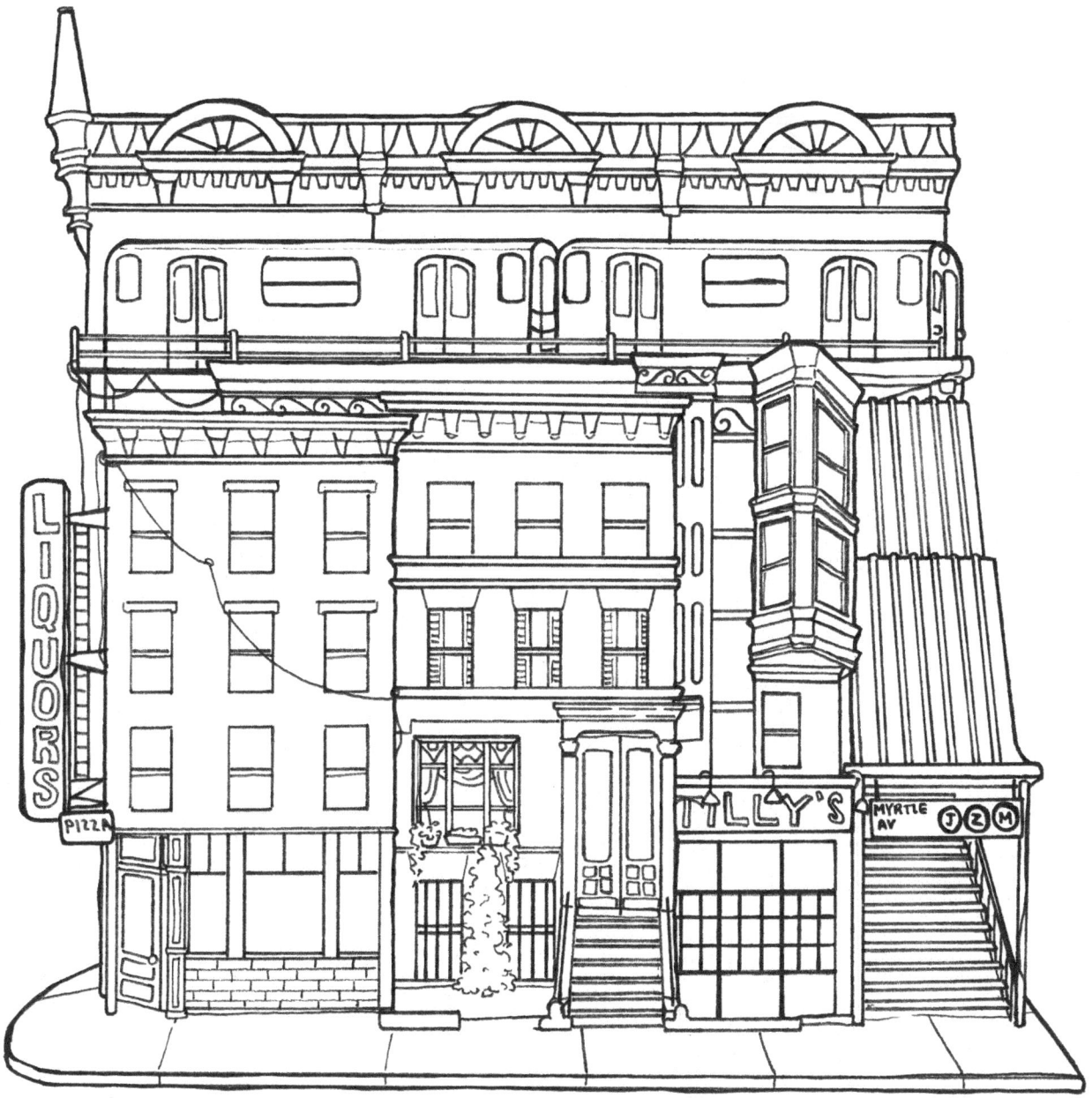
LIQUORS
PIZZA
TILLY'S
MYRTLE AV
J Z M

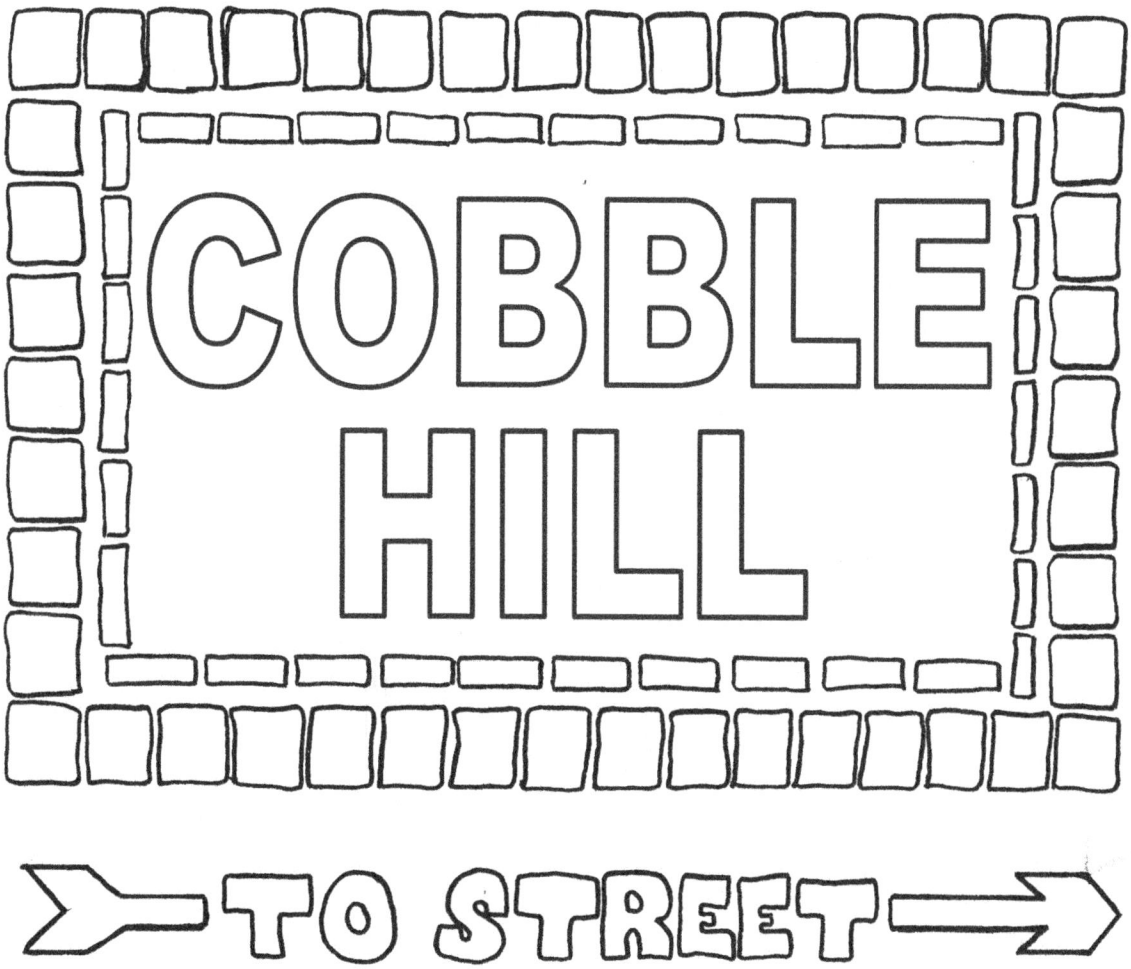
COBBLE
HILL
TO STREET

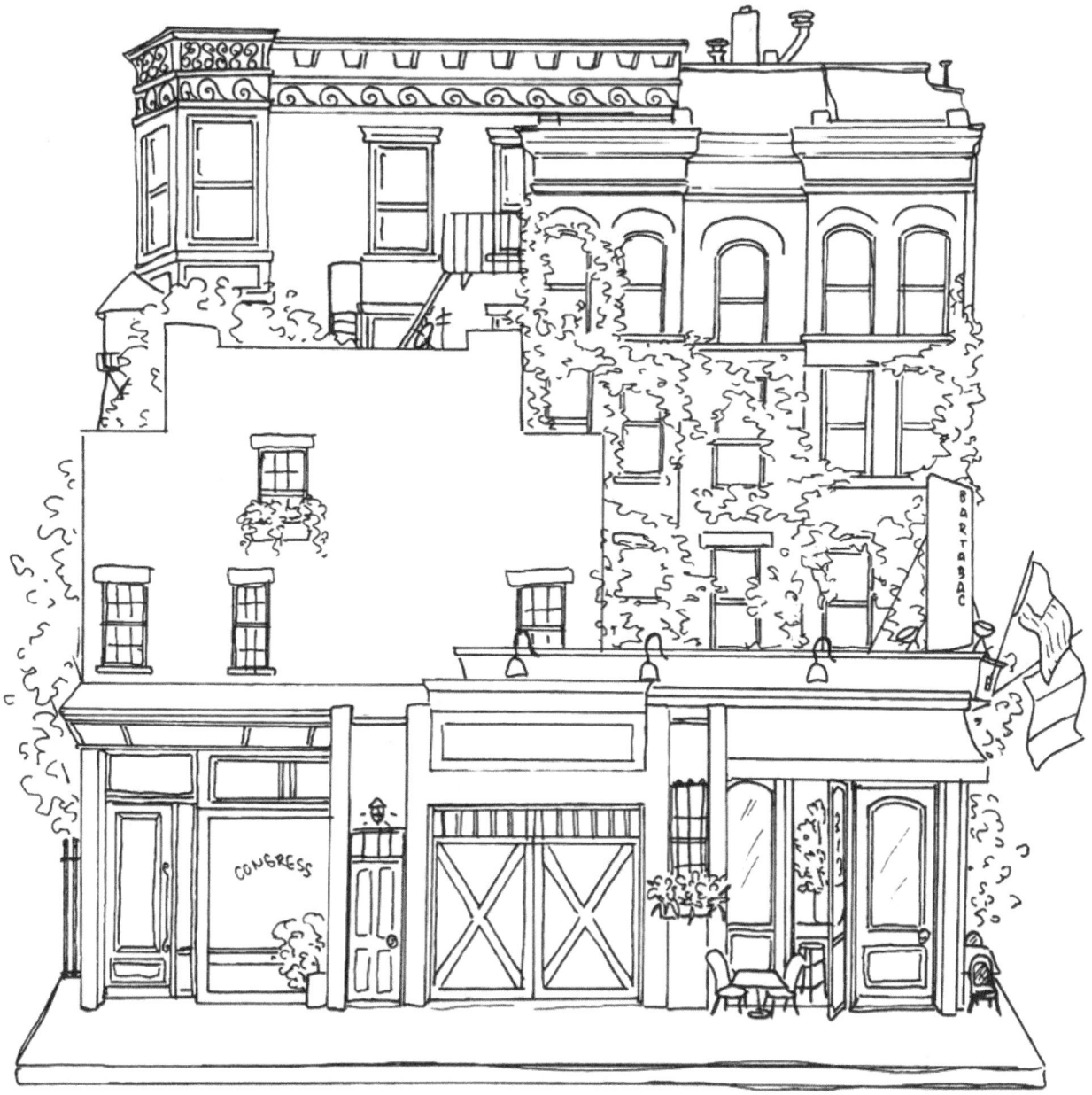
CONGRESS
BARTABAU

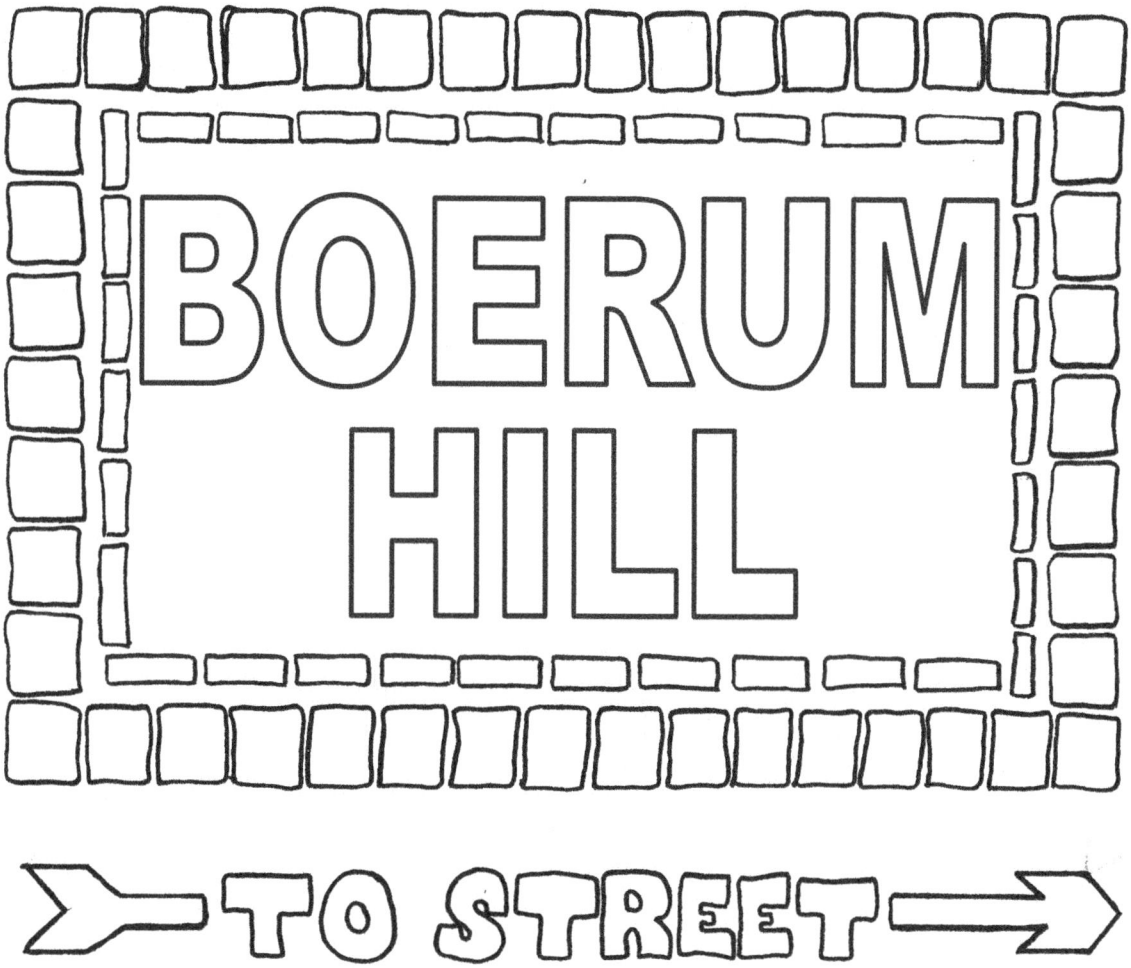
BOERUM
HILL
TO STREET

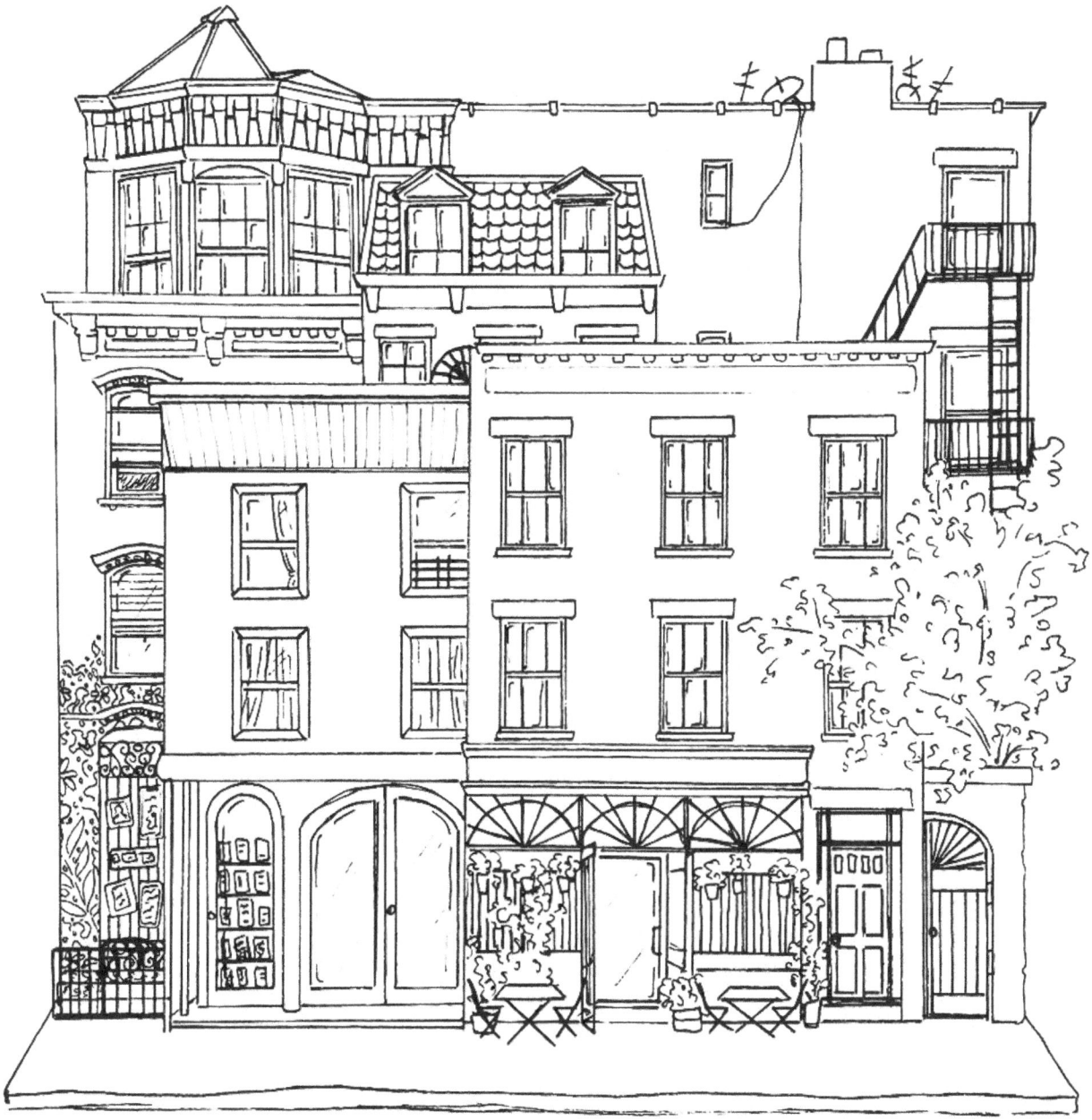

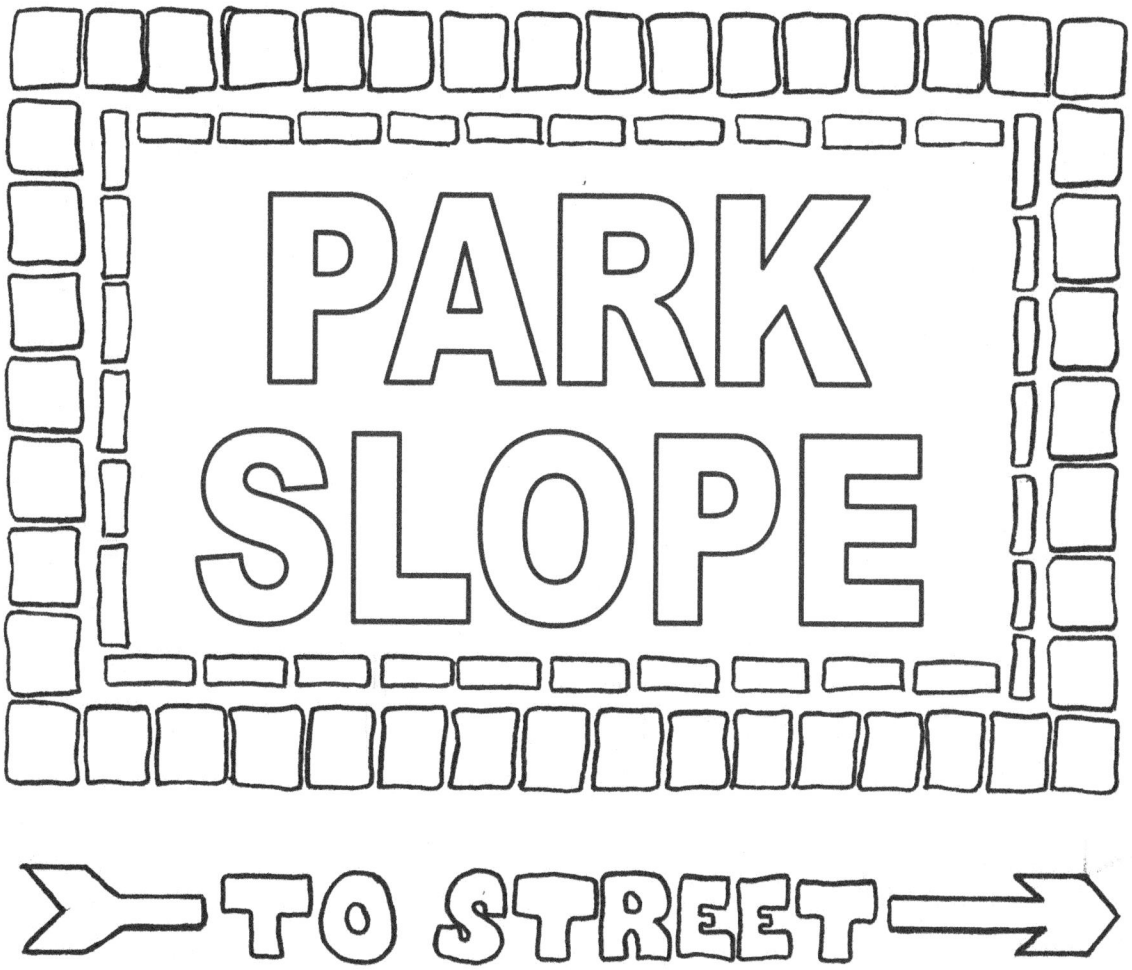
PARK
SLOPE
TO STREET

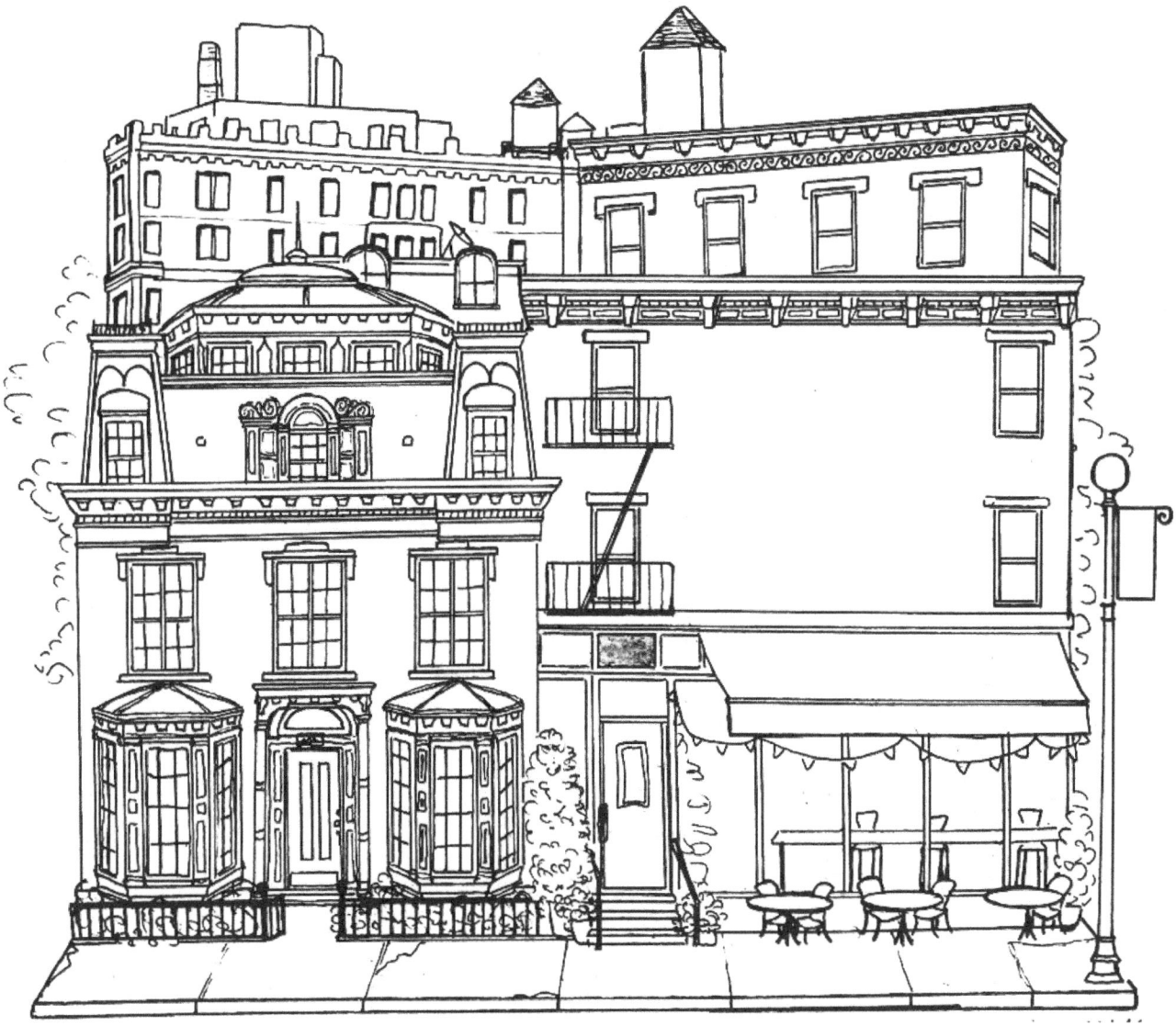

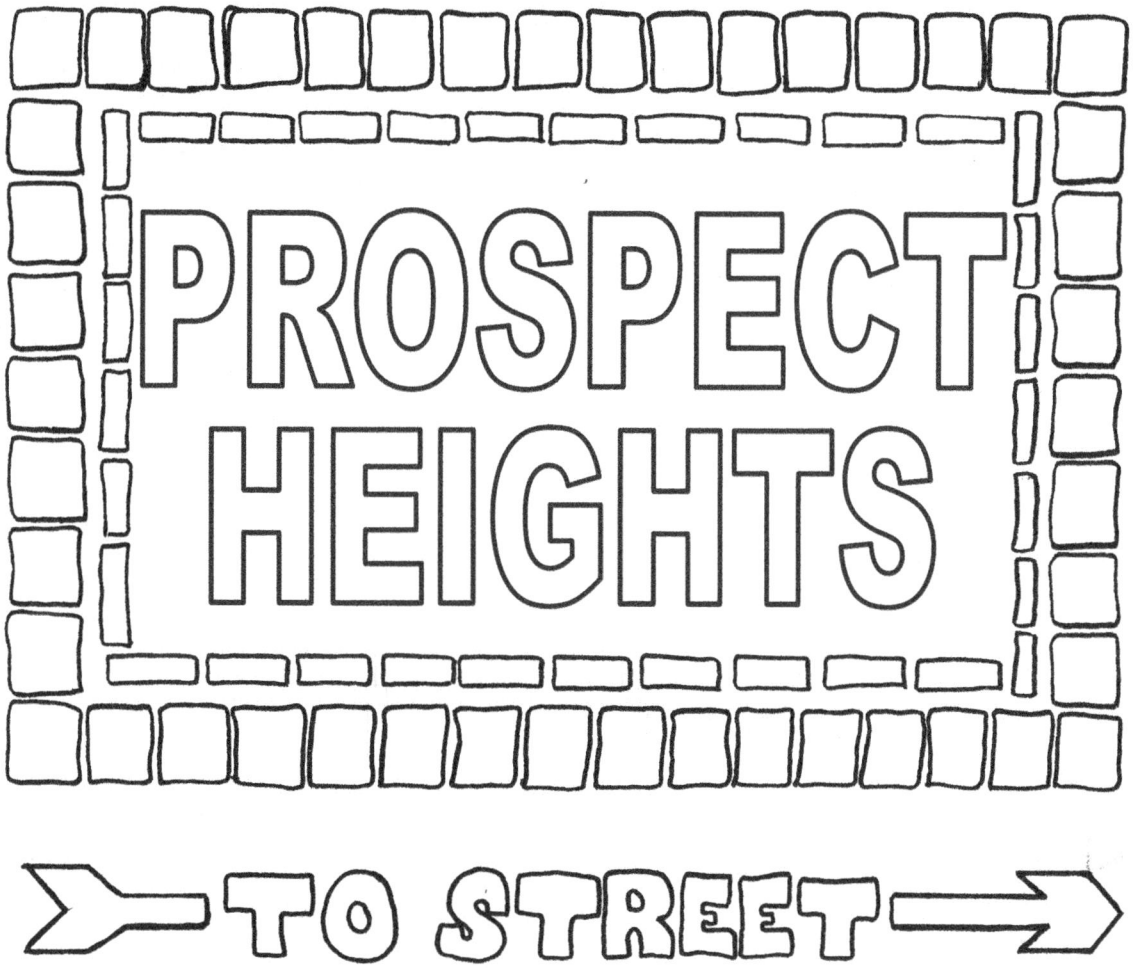
PROSPECT
HEIGHTS
TO STREET

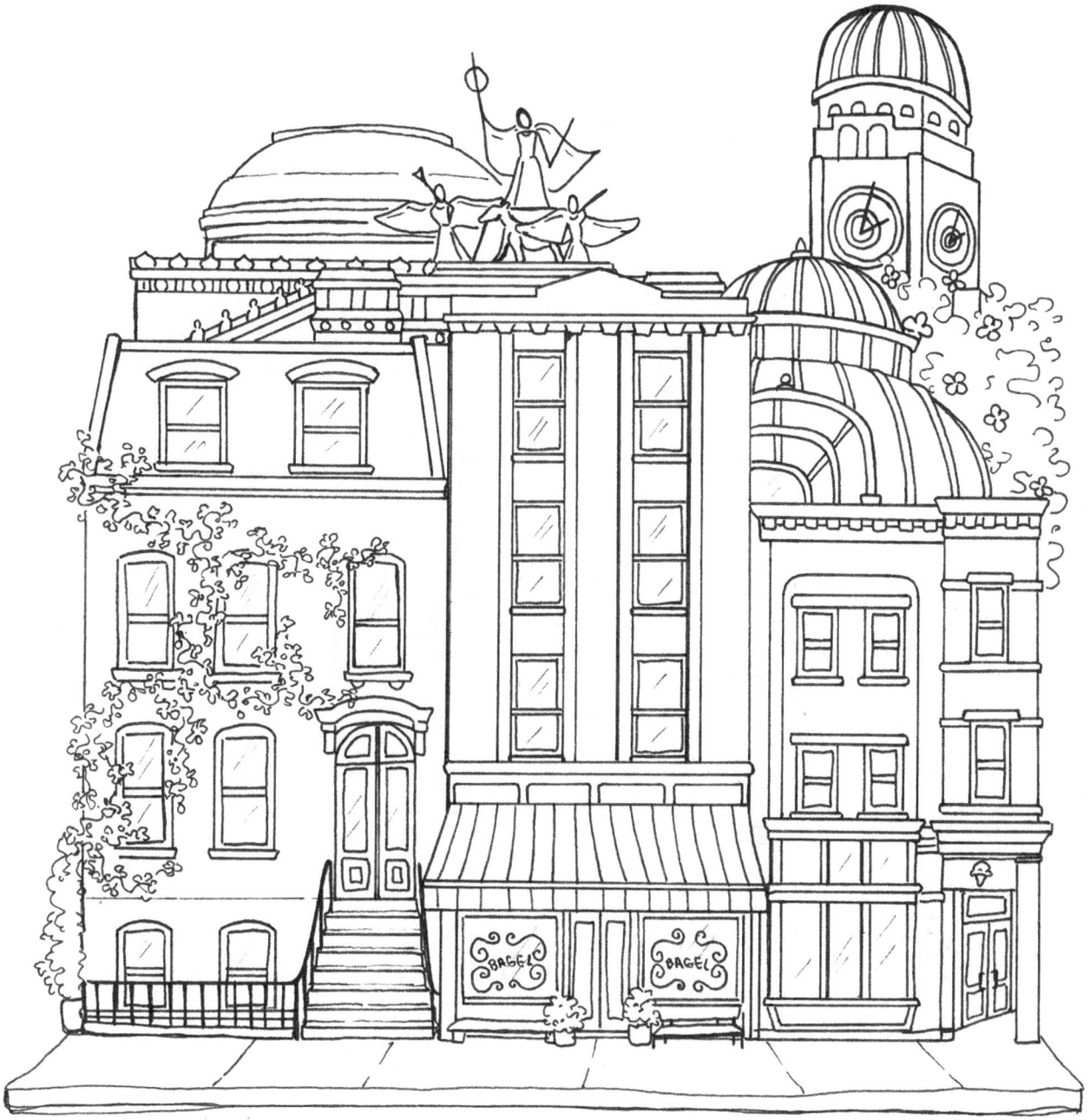
BAGEL
BAGEL

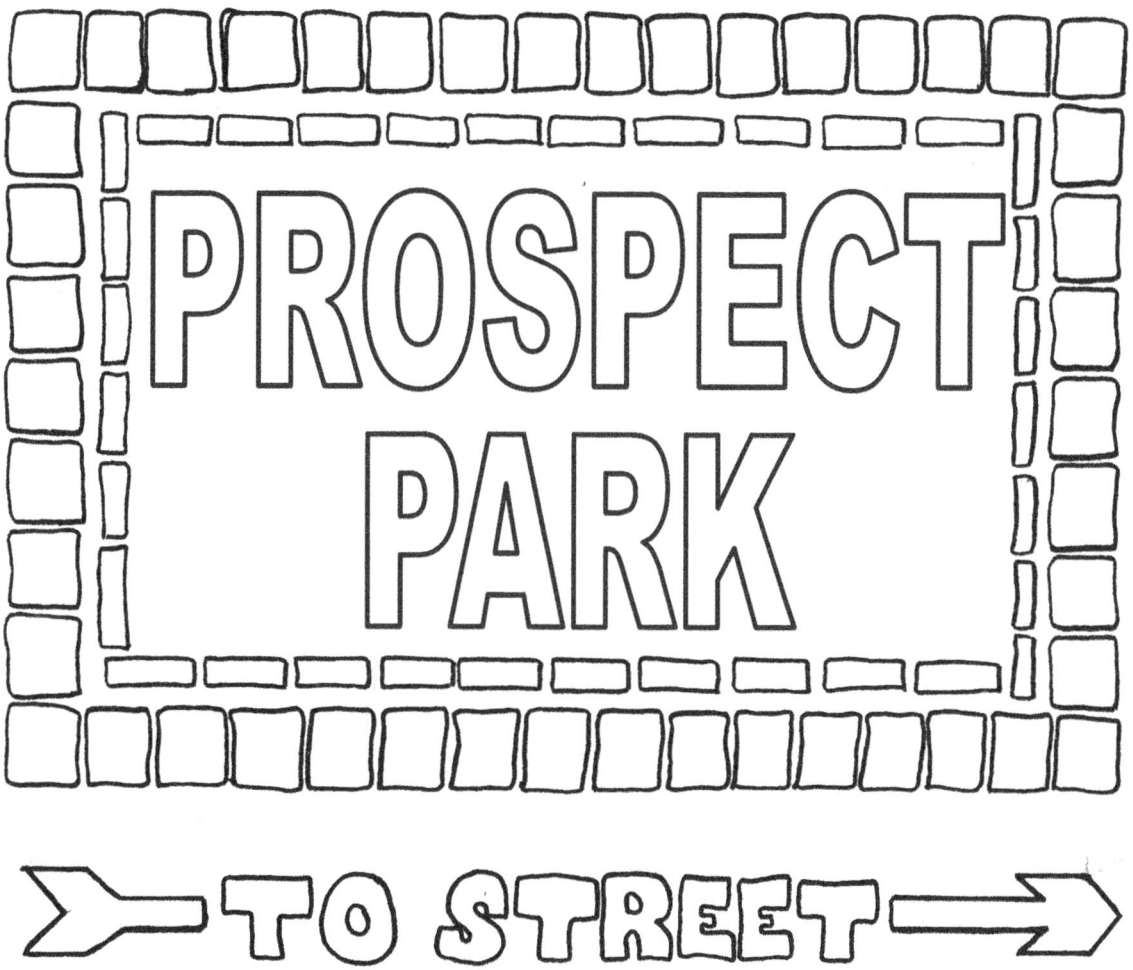
PROSPECT
PARK
TO STREET

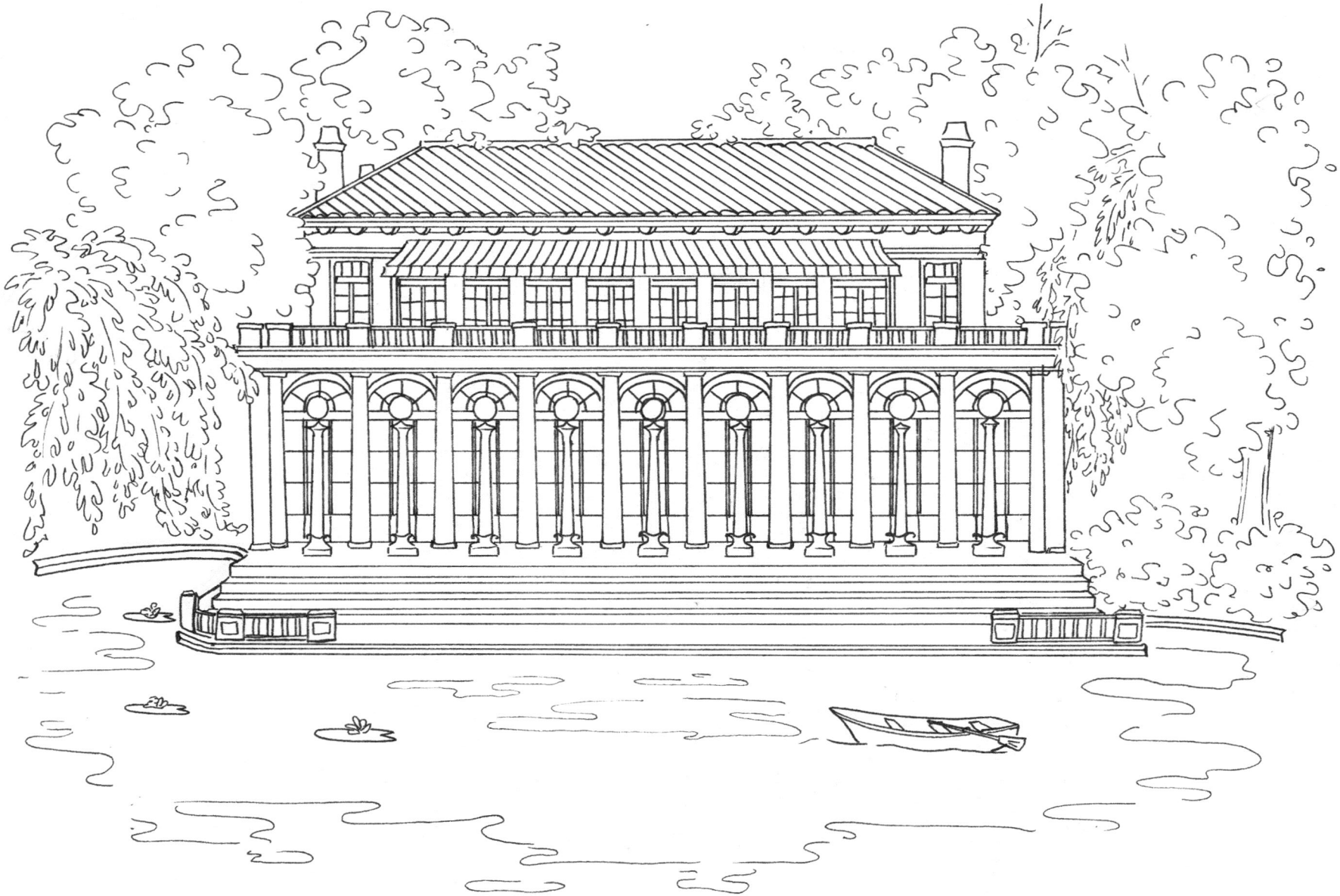

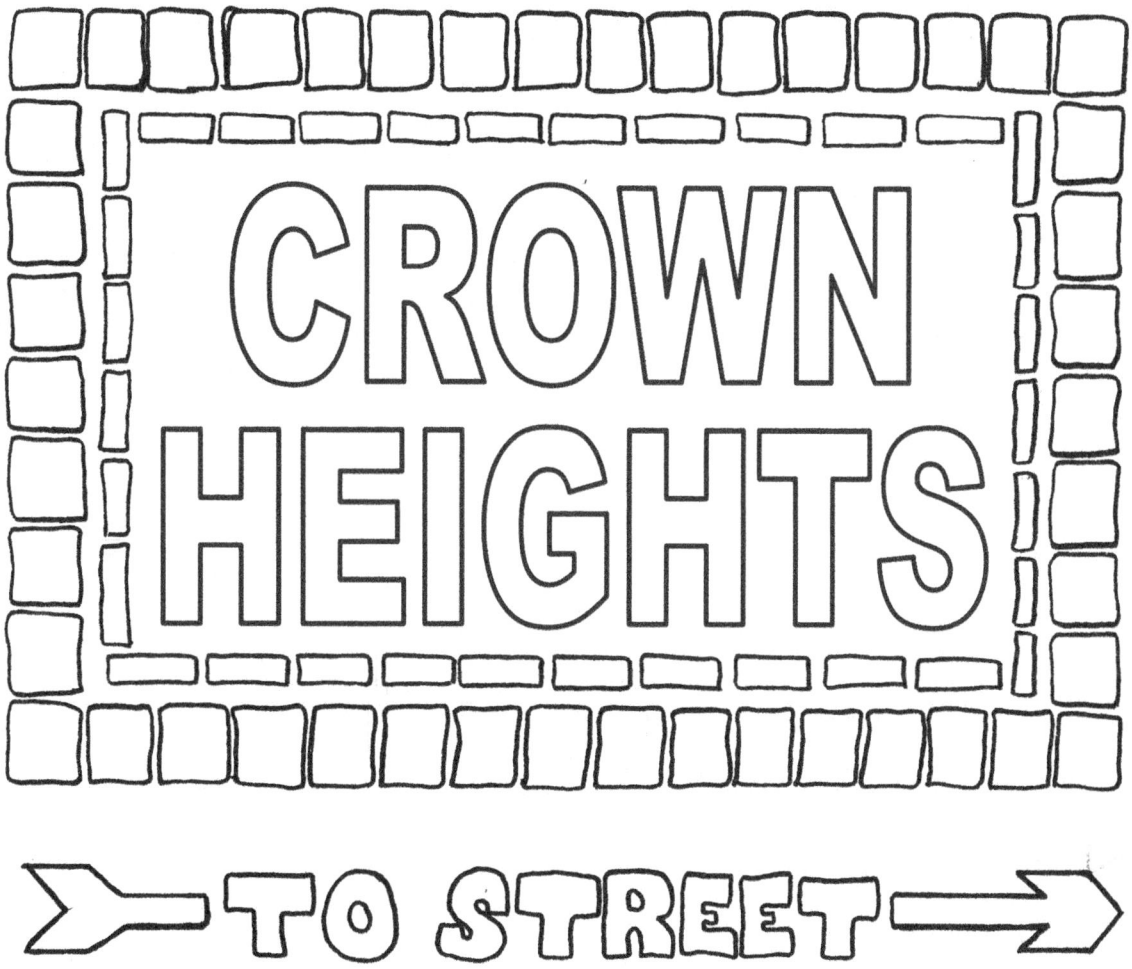
CROWN
HEIGHTS
TO STREET

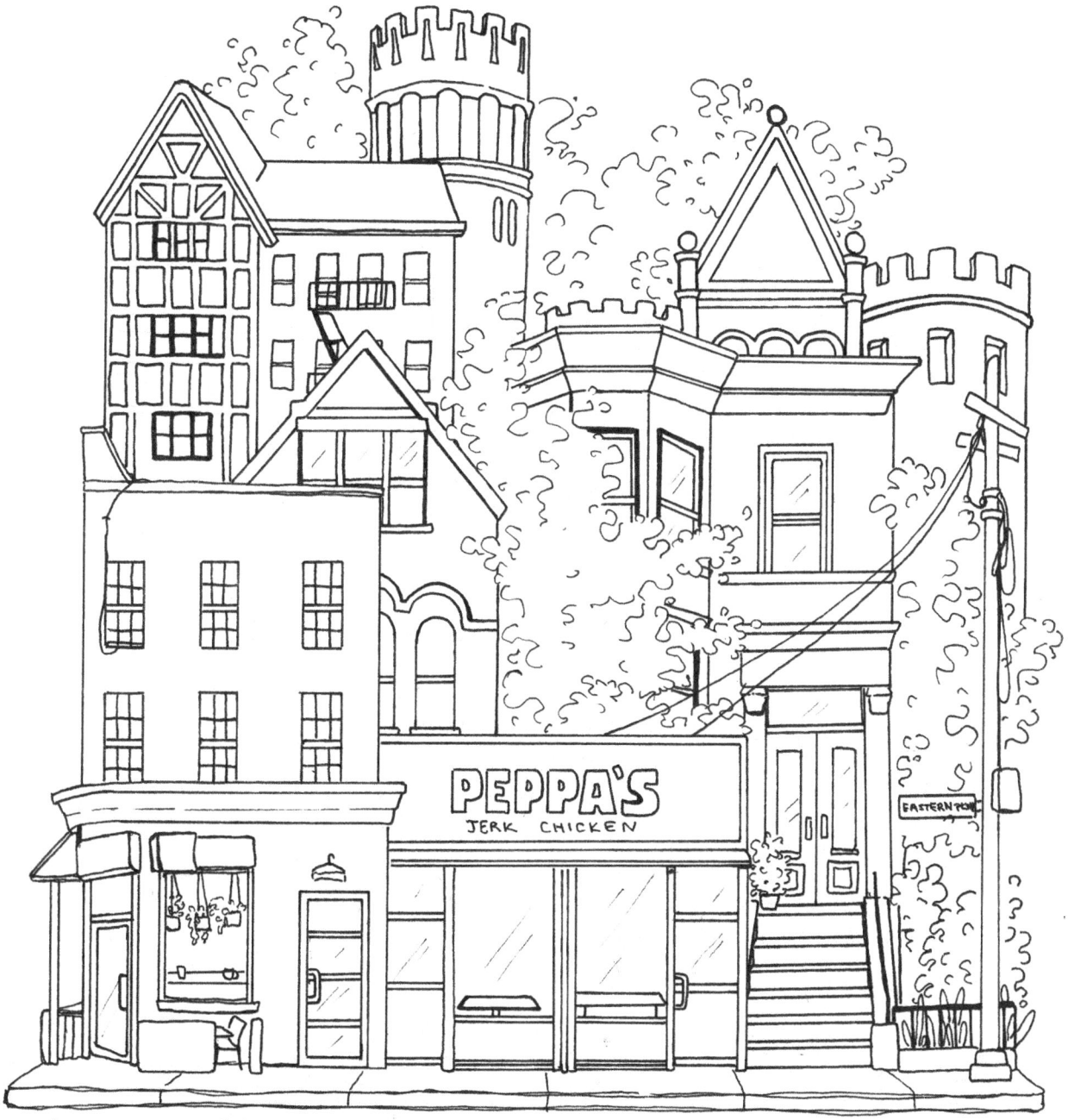
PEPPA'S
JERK CHICKEN
EASTERN PKWY

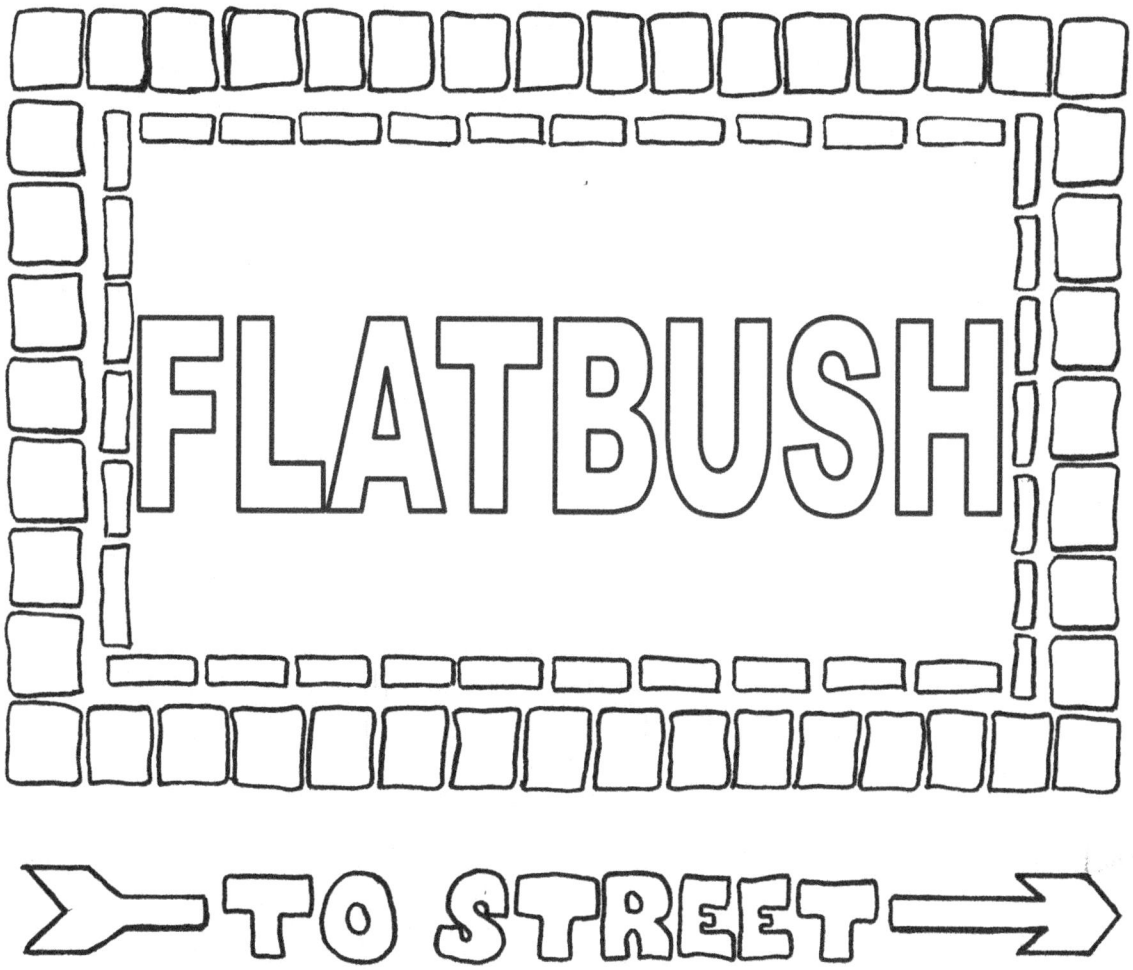
FLATBUSH
TO STREET

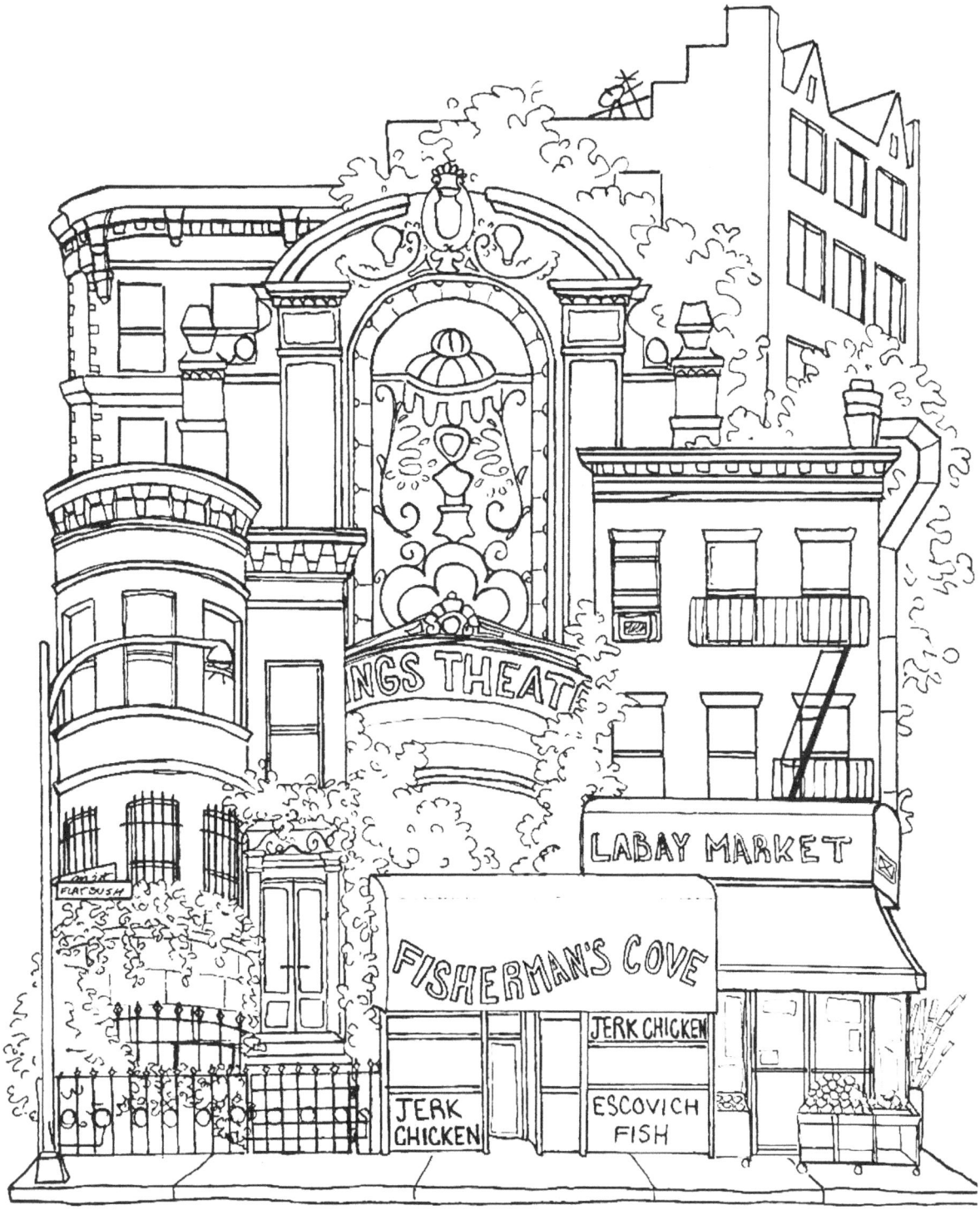
NGS THEAT
LABAY MARKET
FISHERMAN'S COVE
JERK CHICKEN
JERK CHICKEN
ESCOVICH FISH

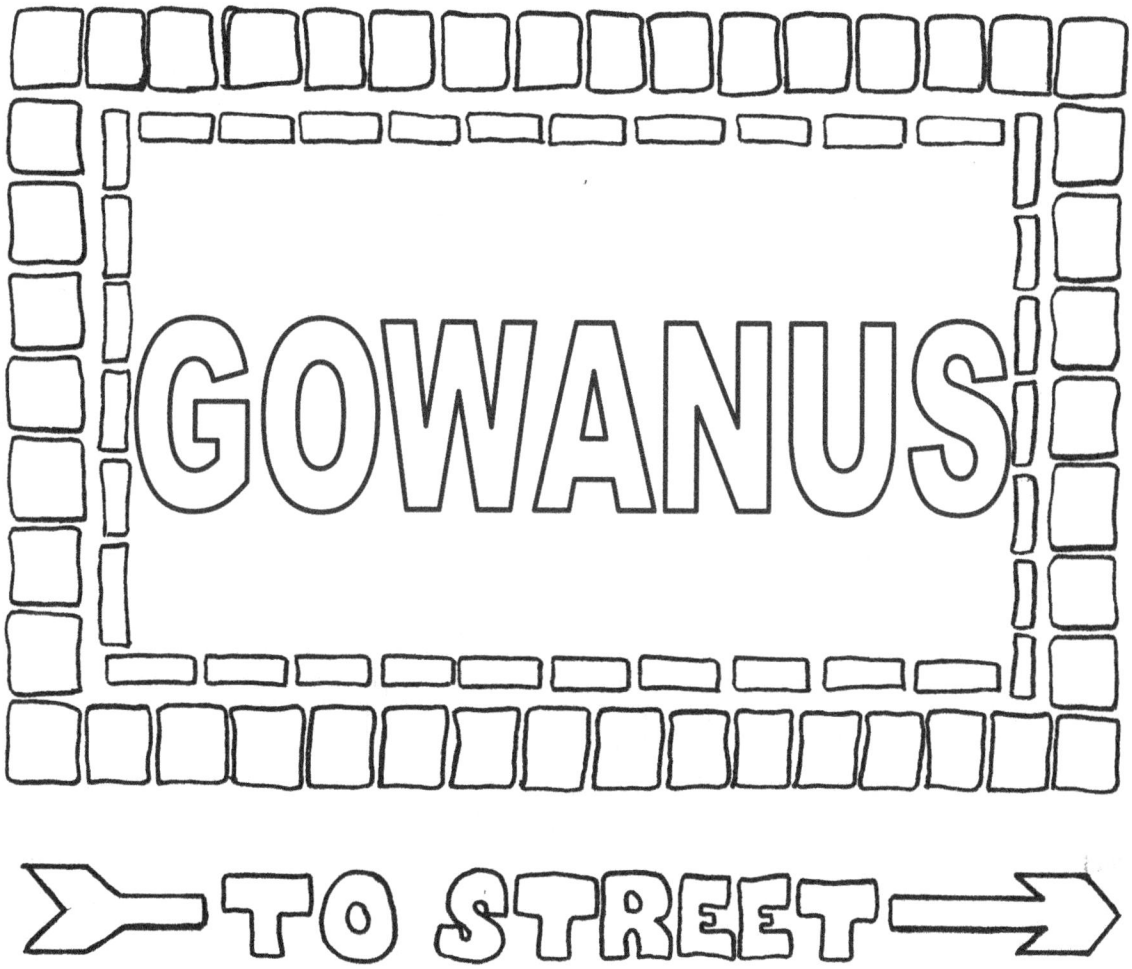
GOWANUS
TO STREET

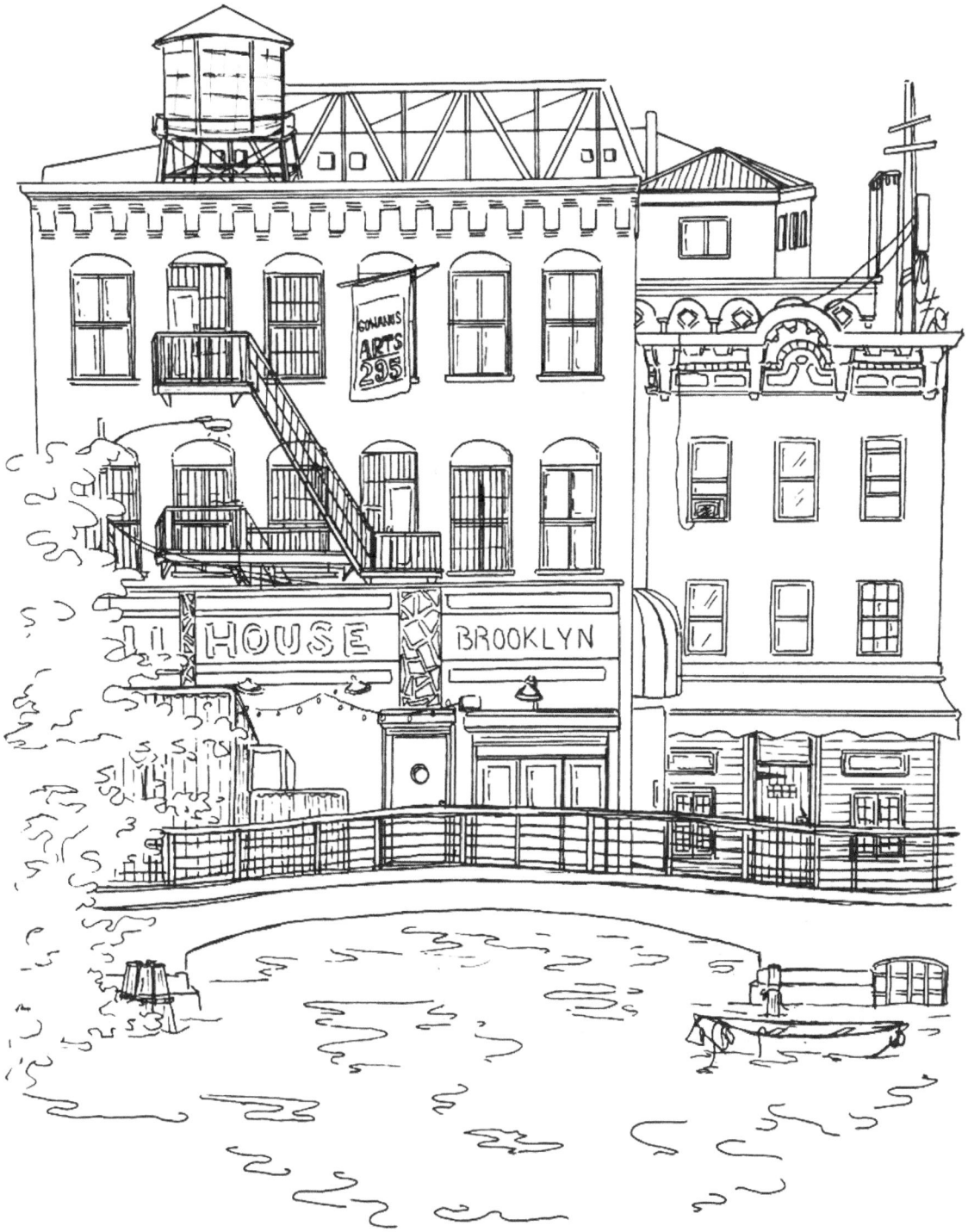
GOWANUS
ARTS
295
HOUSE
BROOKLYN

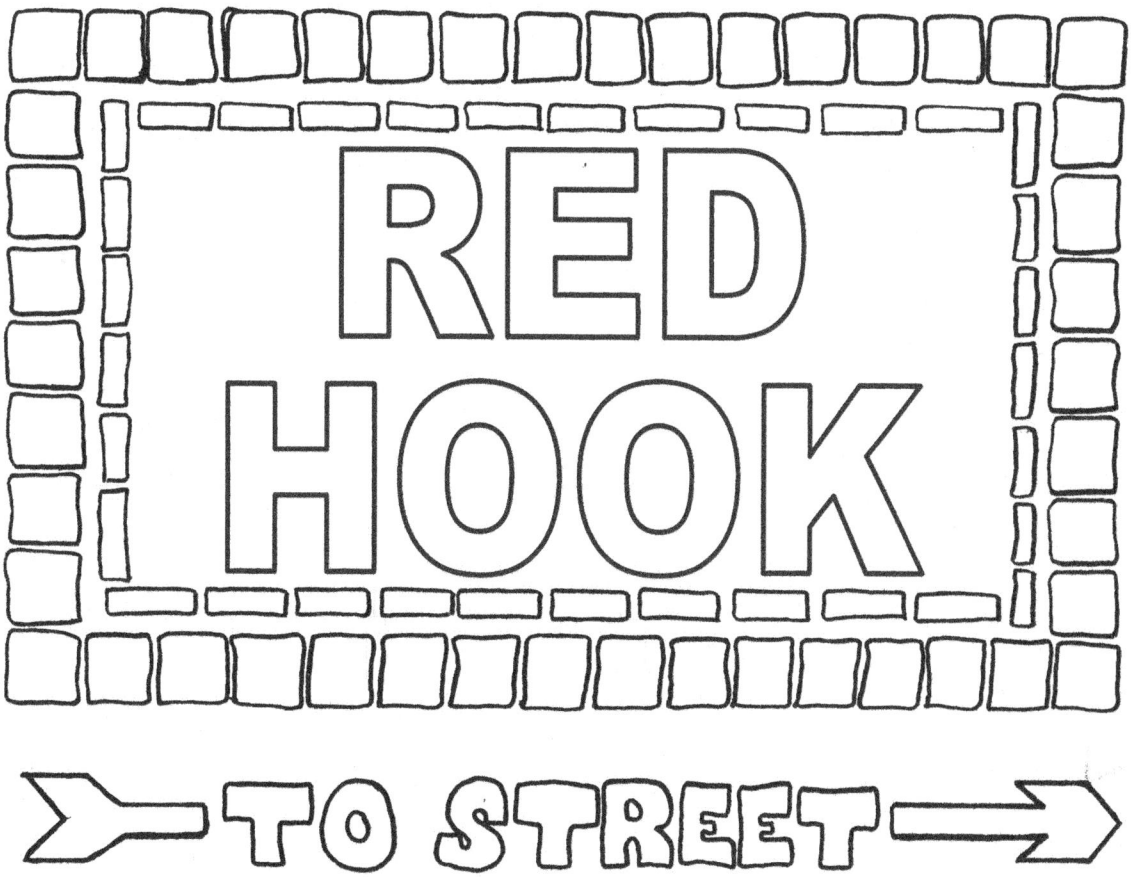
RED
HOOK
TO STREET

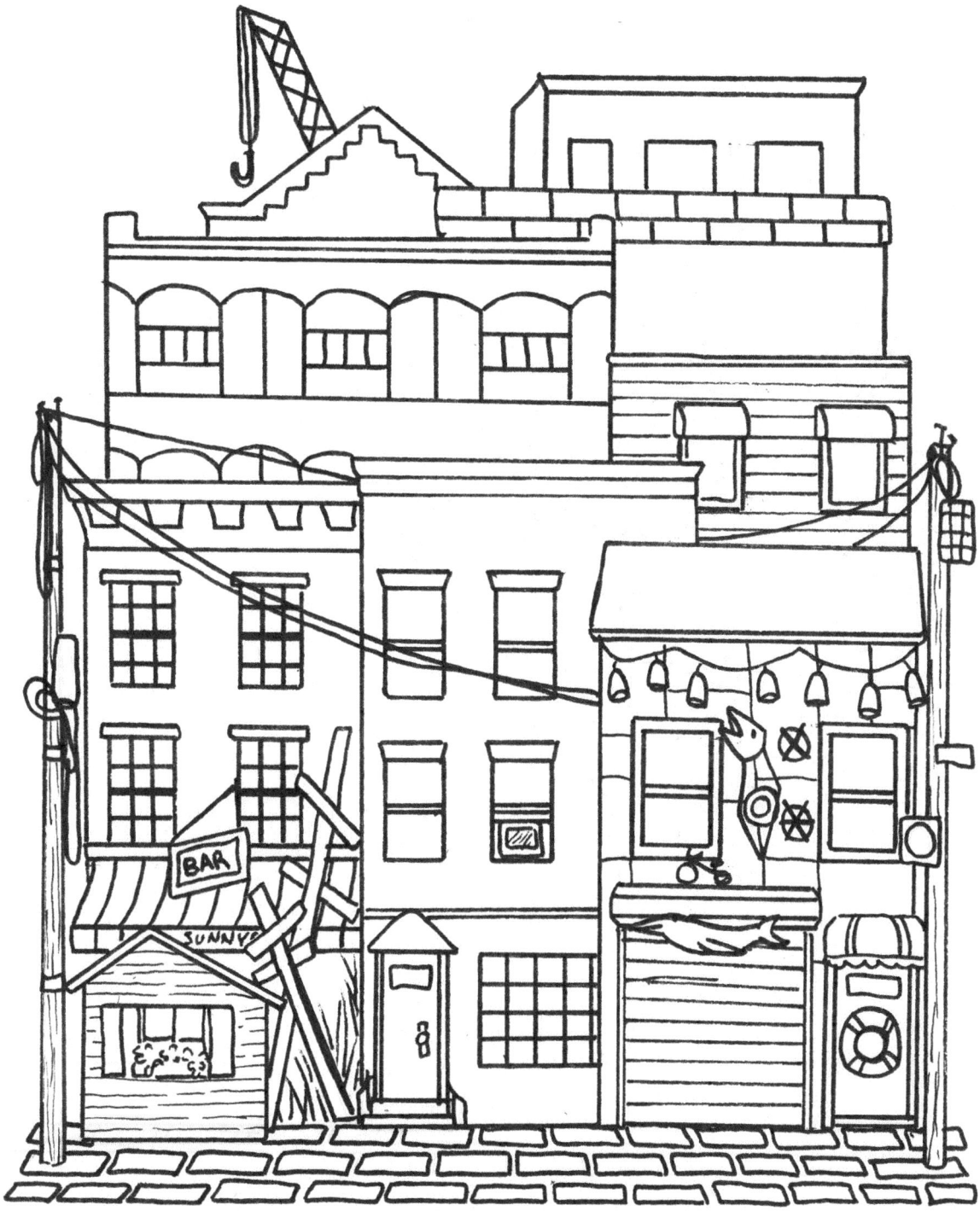
BAR
SUNNY'S

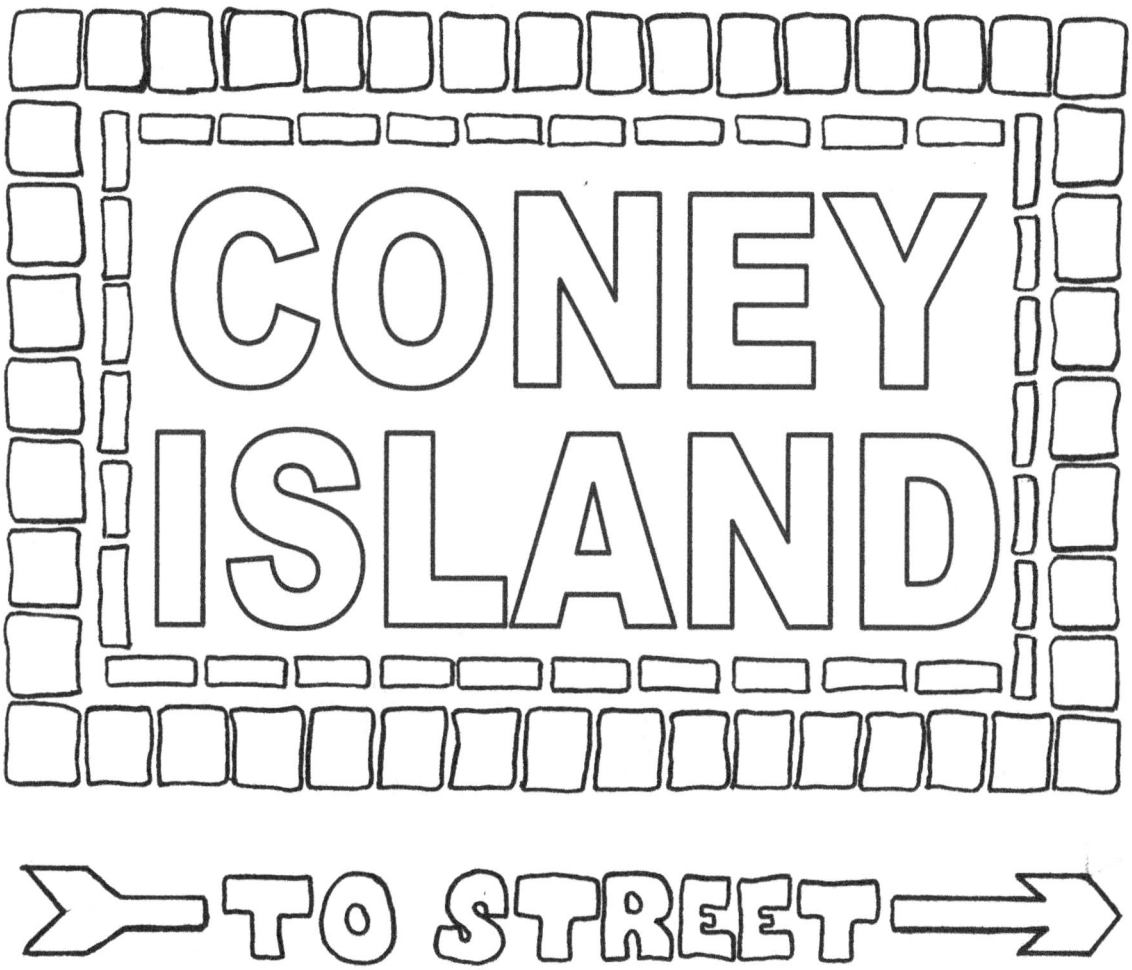
CONEY
ISLAND
TO STREET

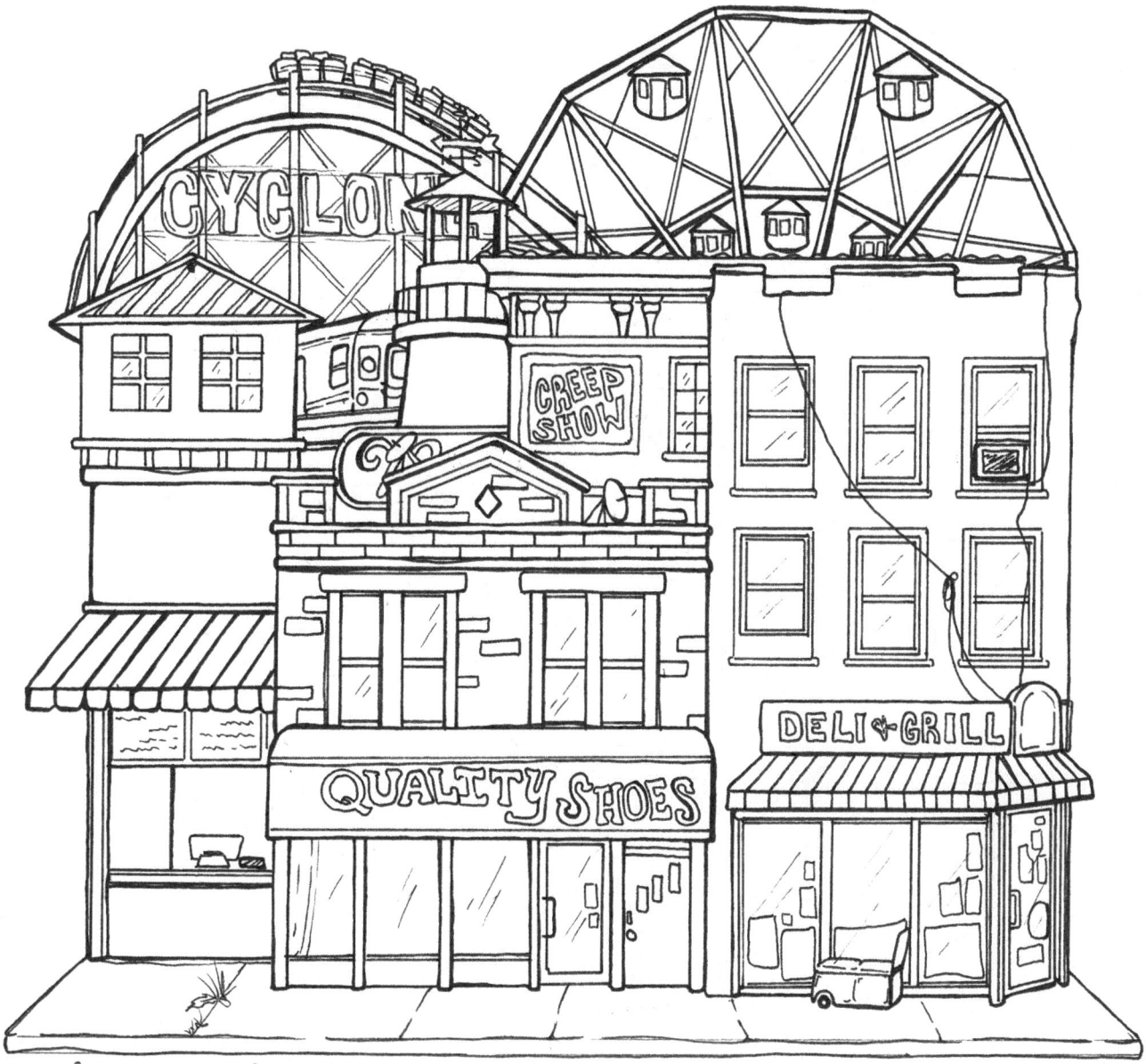
CYCLONE
CREEP SHOW
QUALITY SHOES
DELI & GRILL

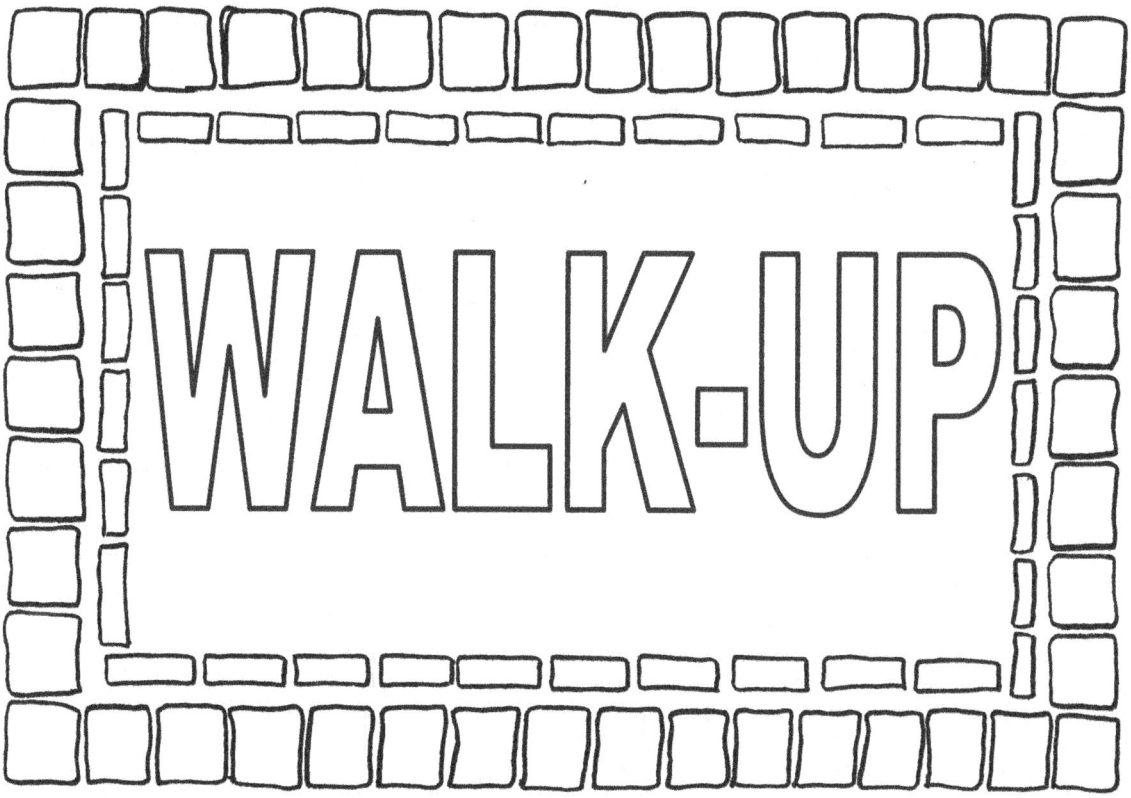
WALK-UP

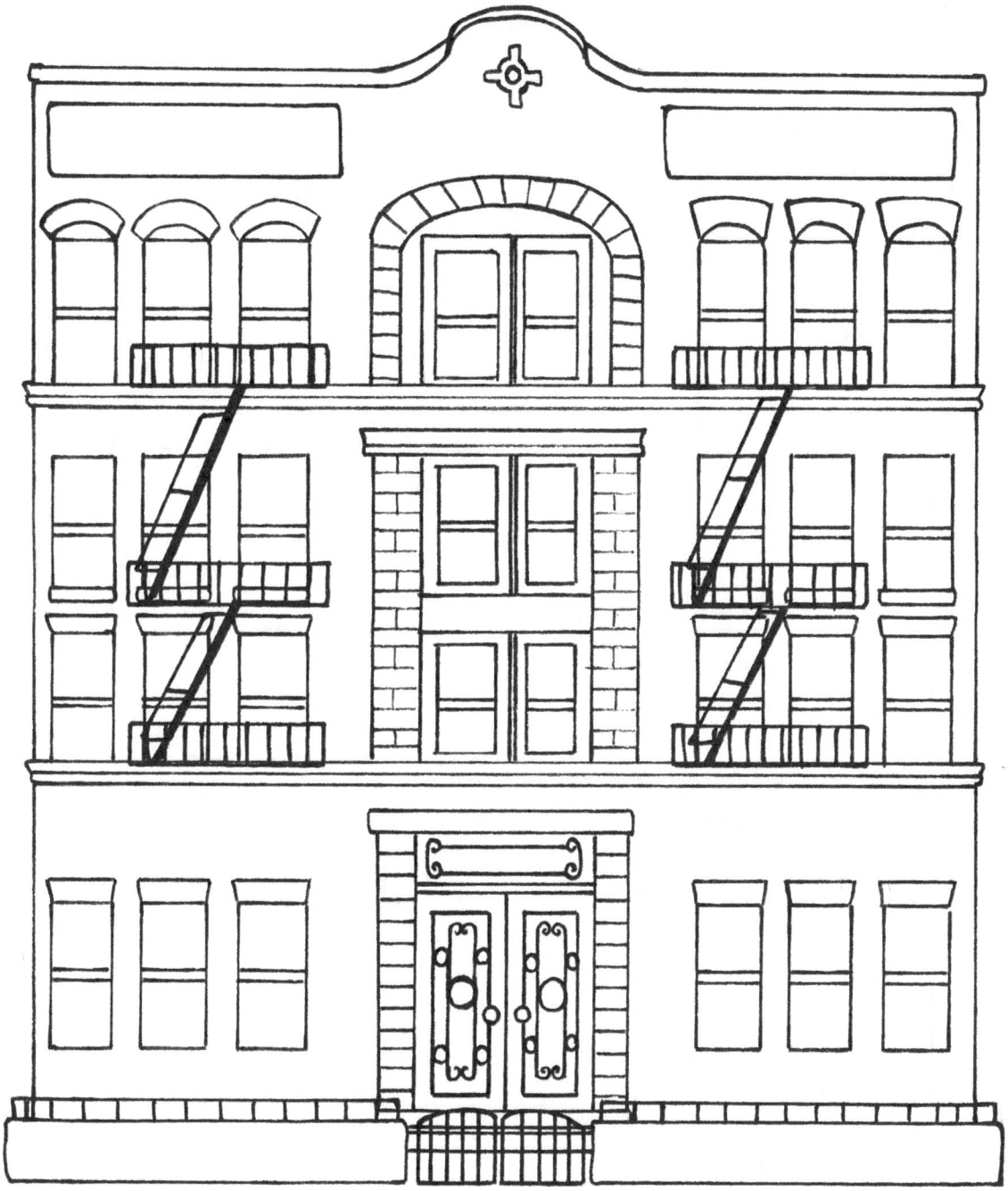

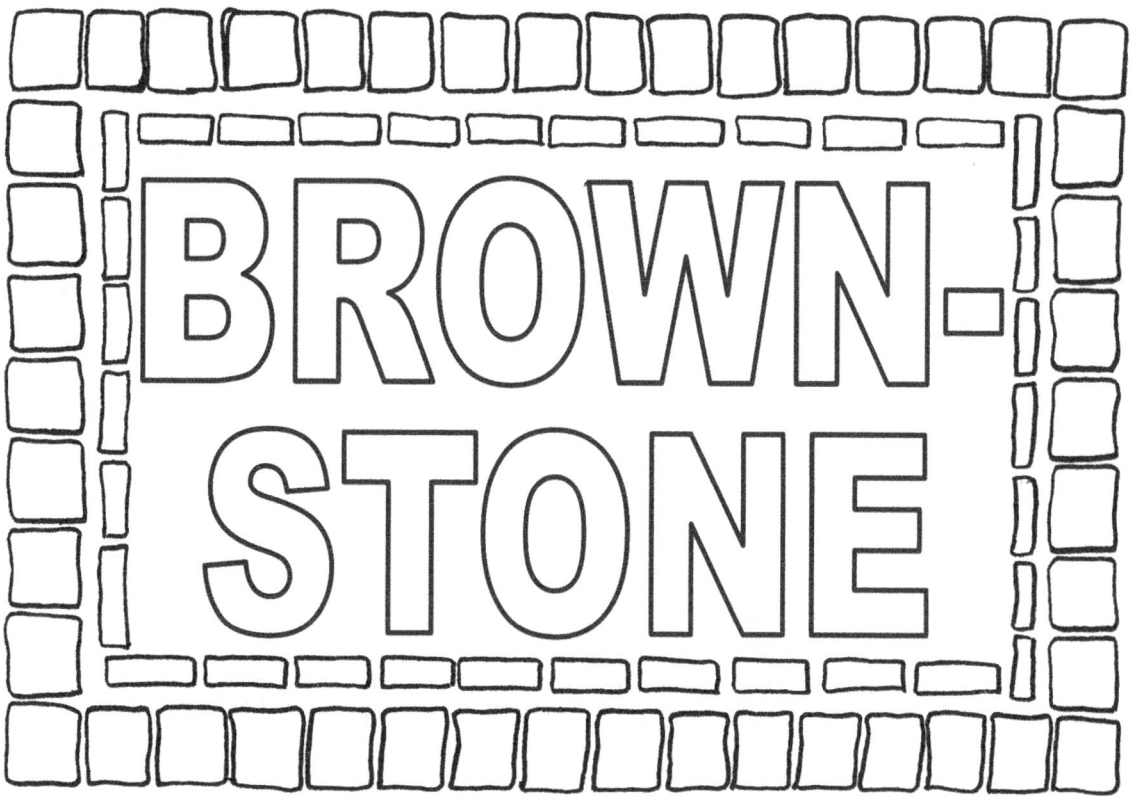
BROWN-
STONE

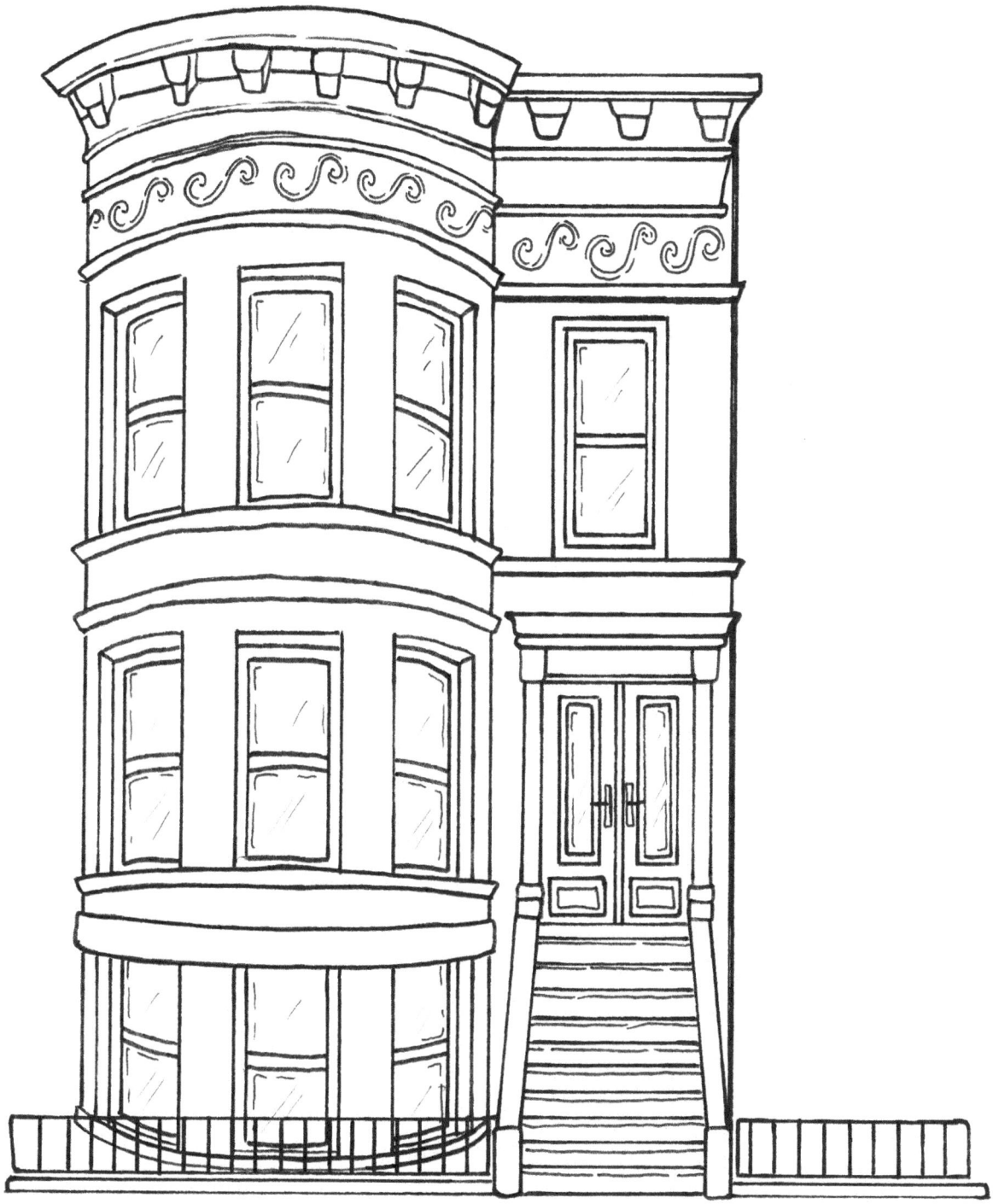

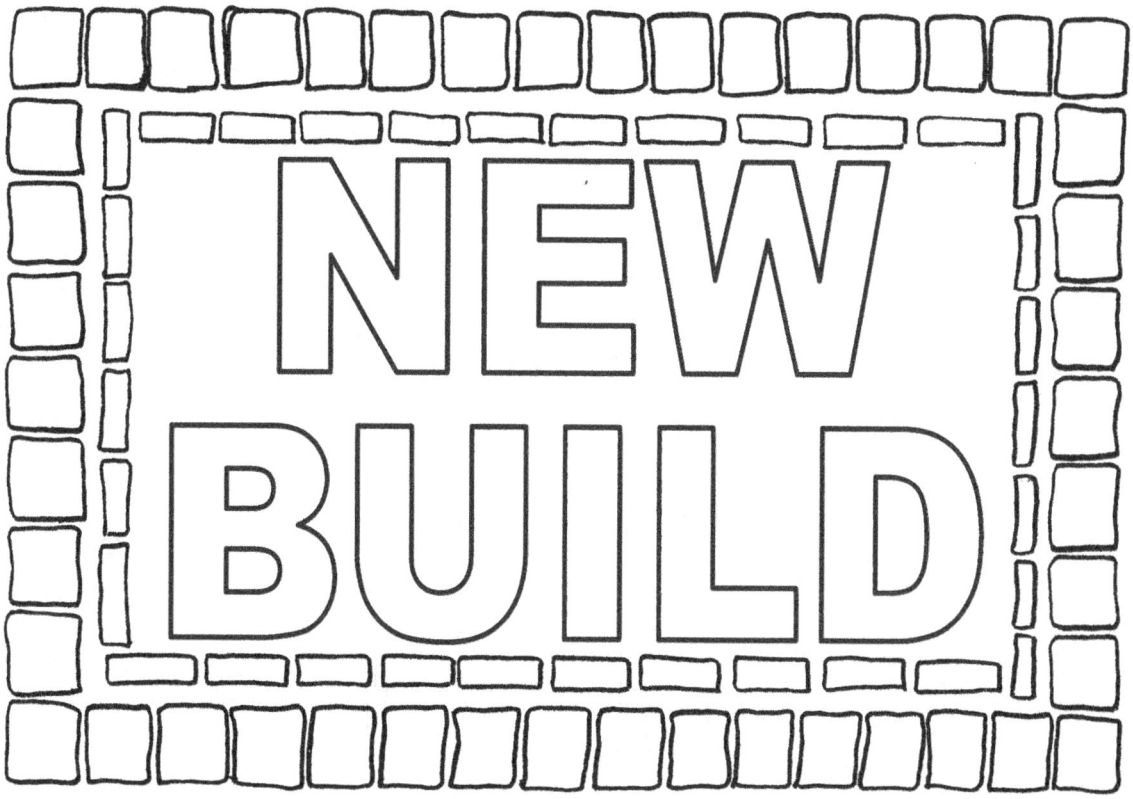
NEW
BUILD

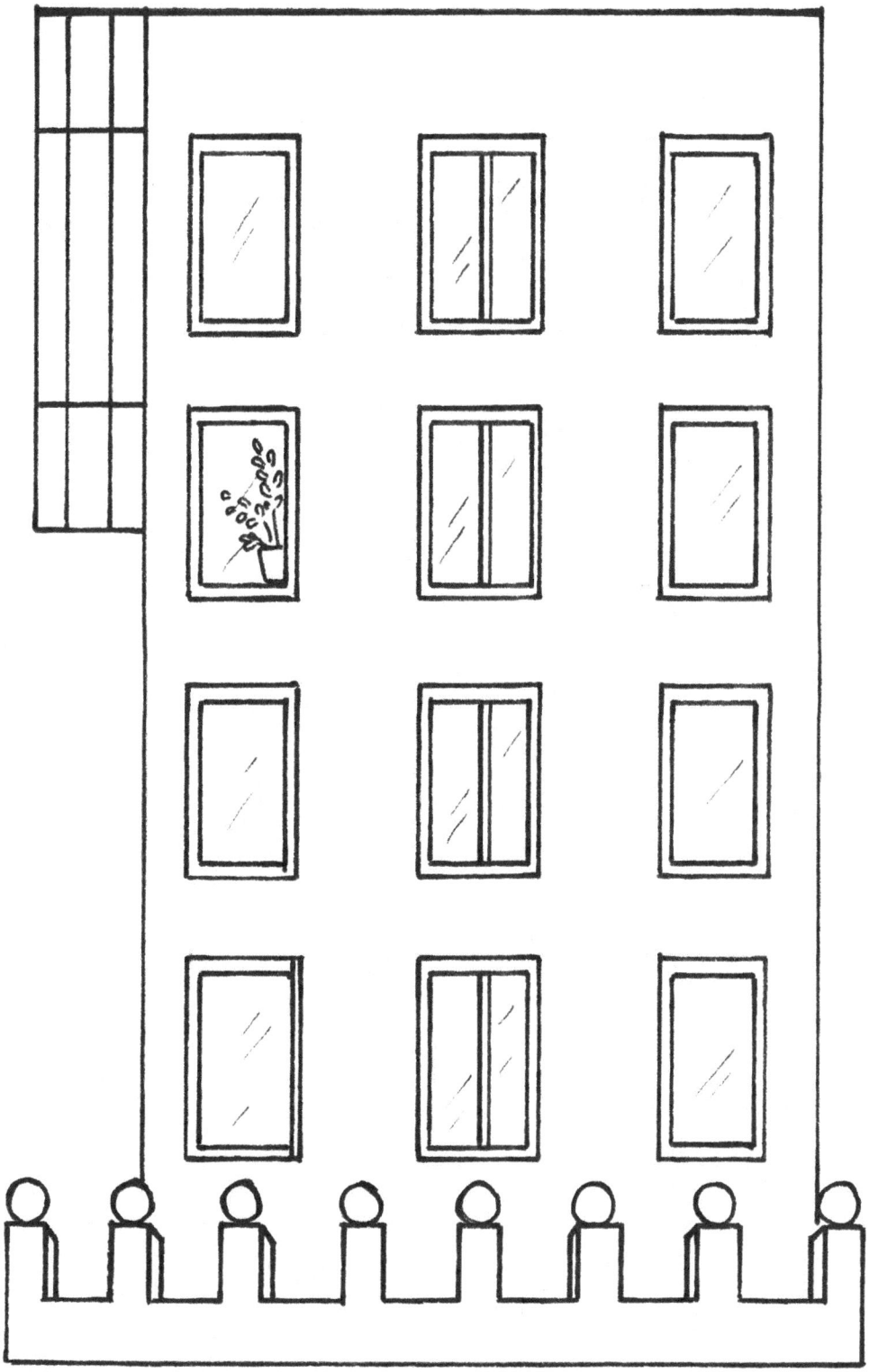

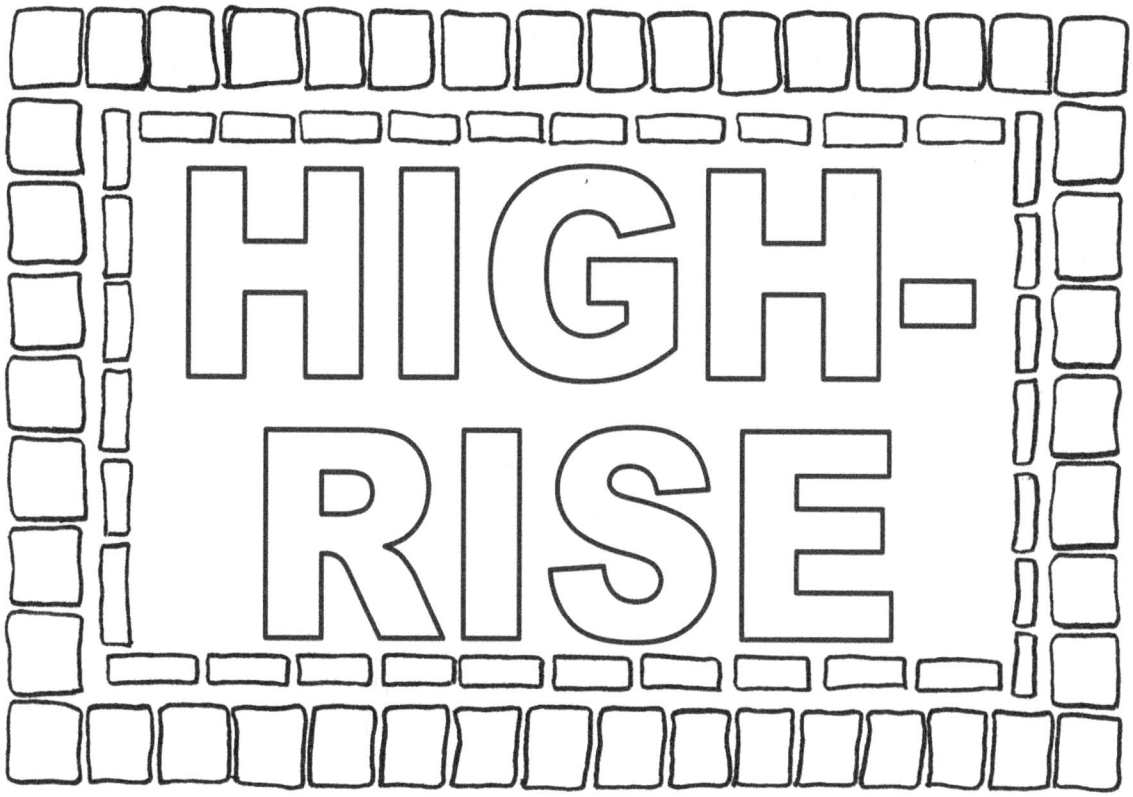
HIGH-
RISE

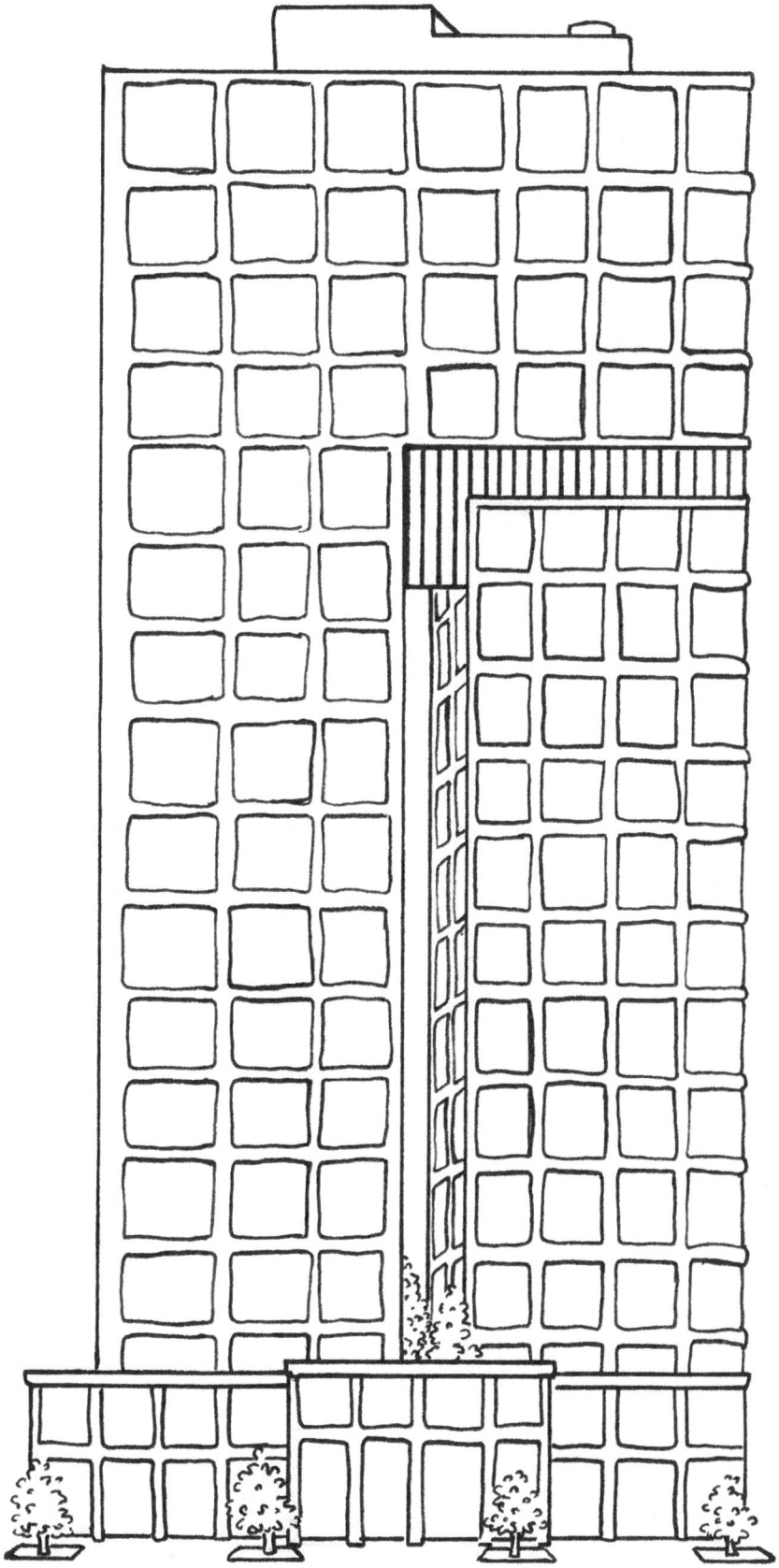

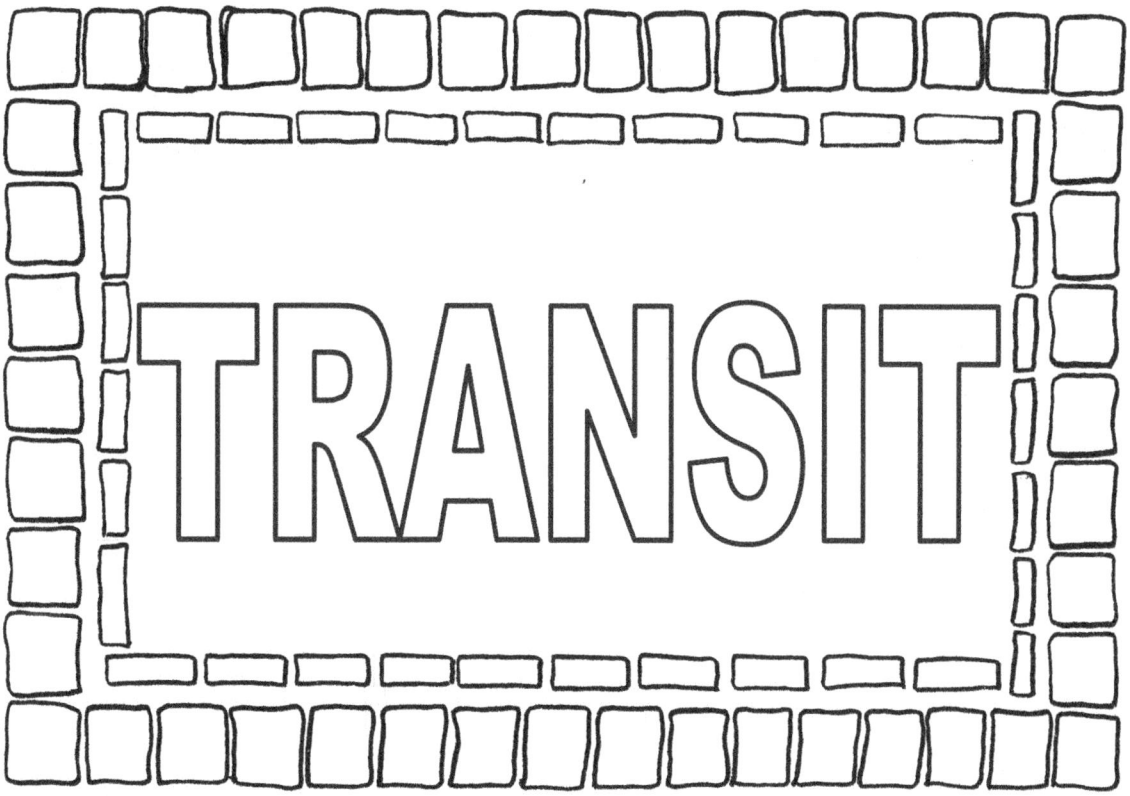
TRANSIT

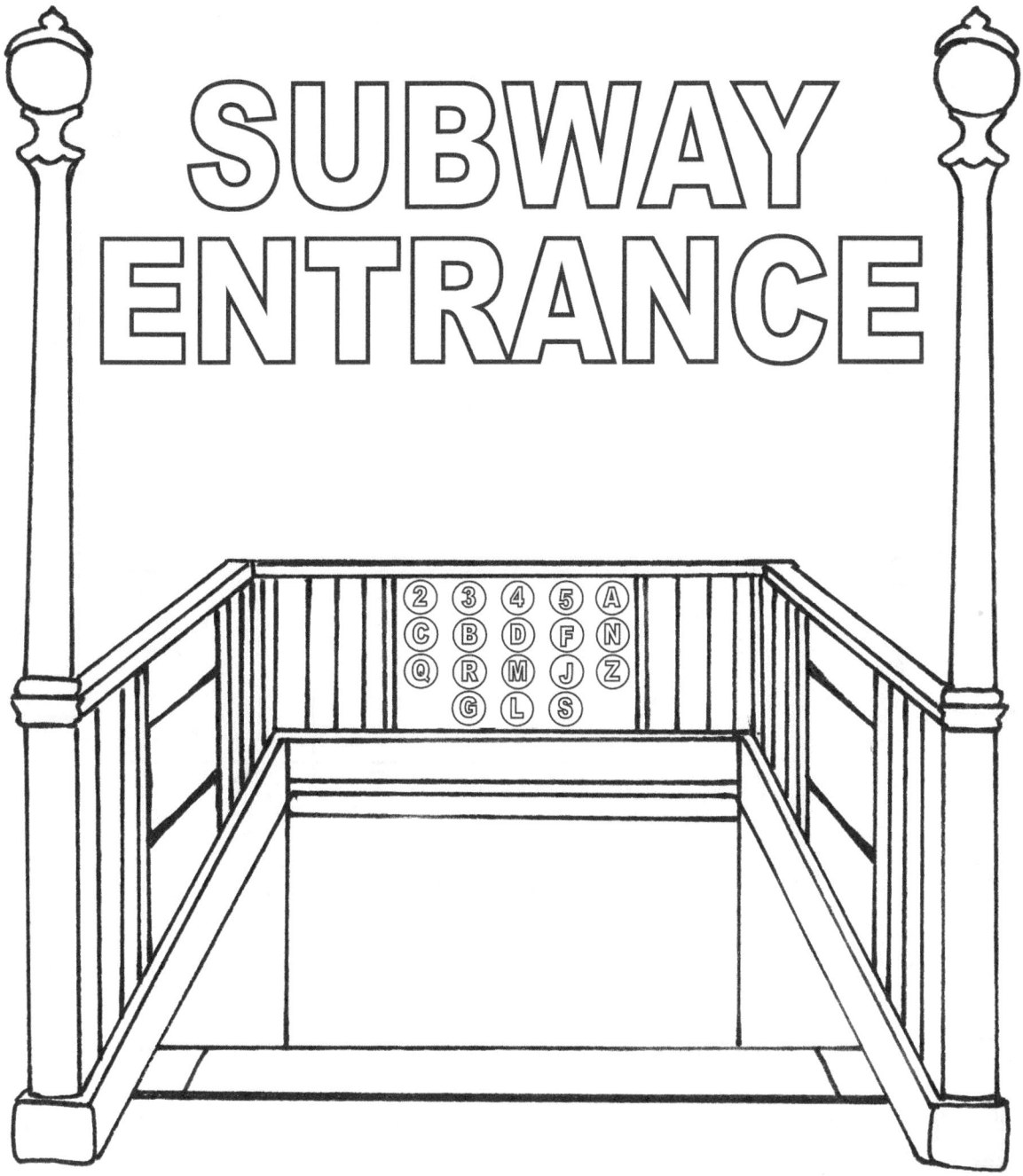
SUBWAY
ENTRANCE
2 3 4 5 A
C B D F N
Q R M J Z
G L S

ELEVATED TRACK

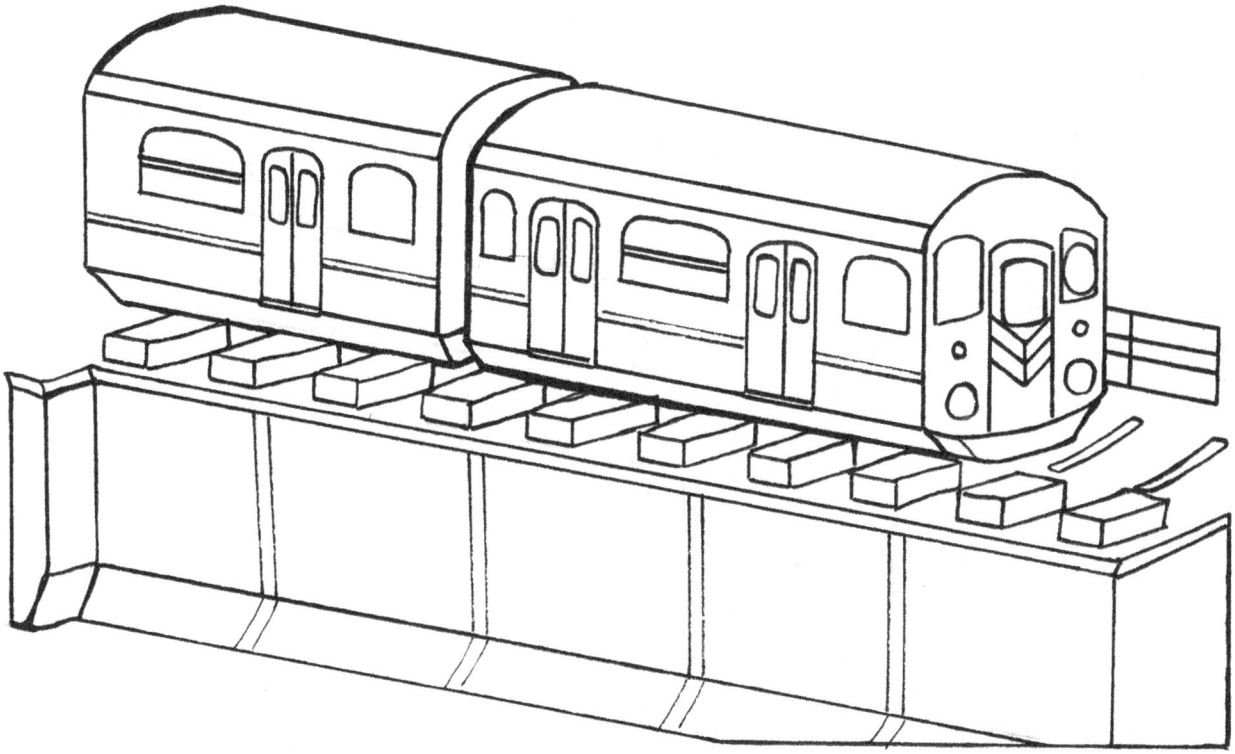

FERRY

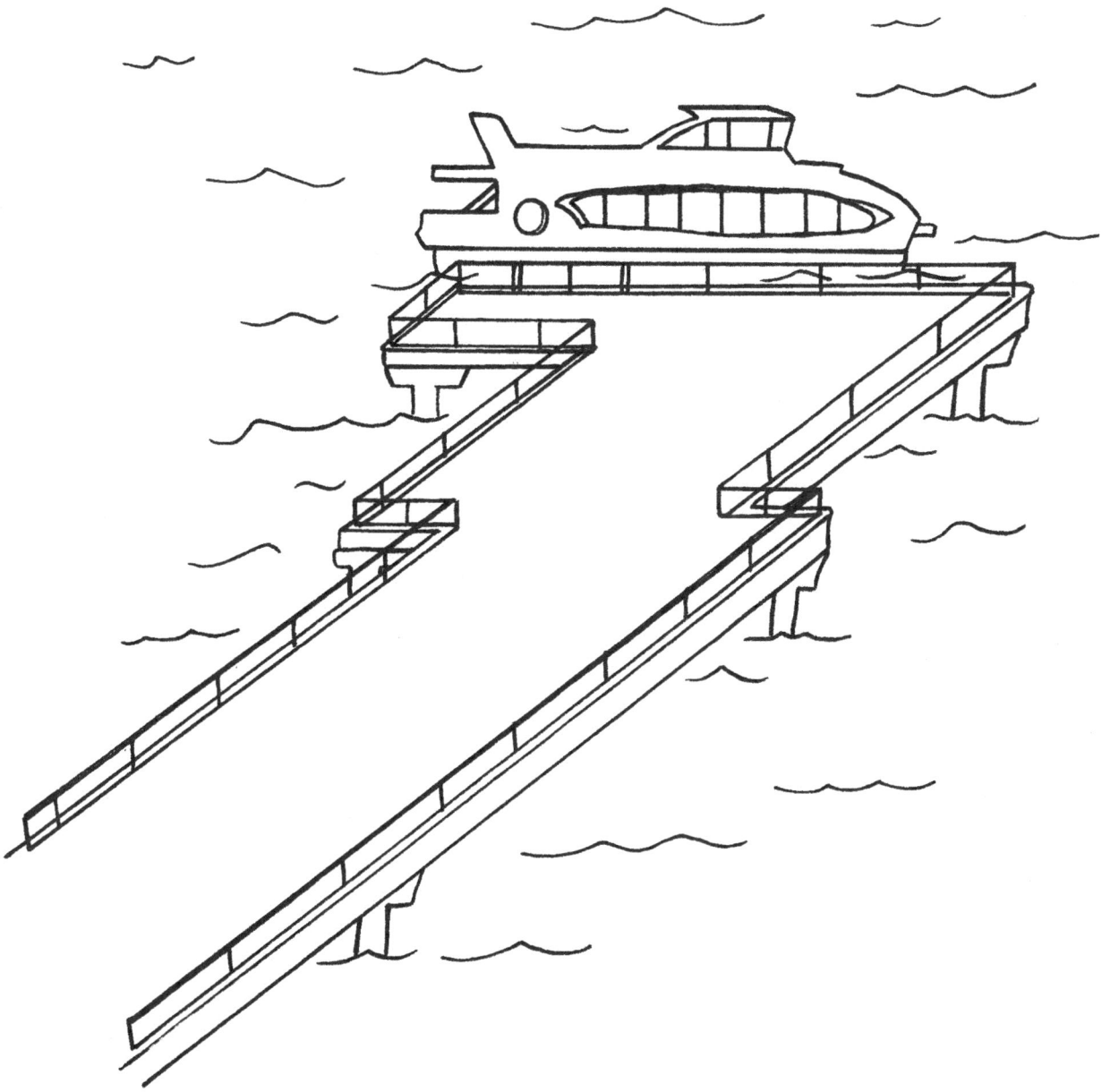

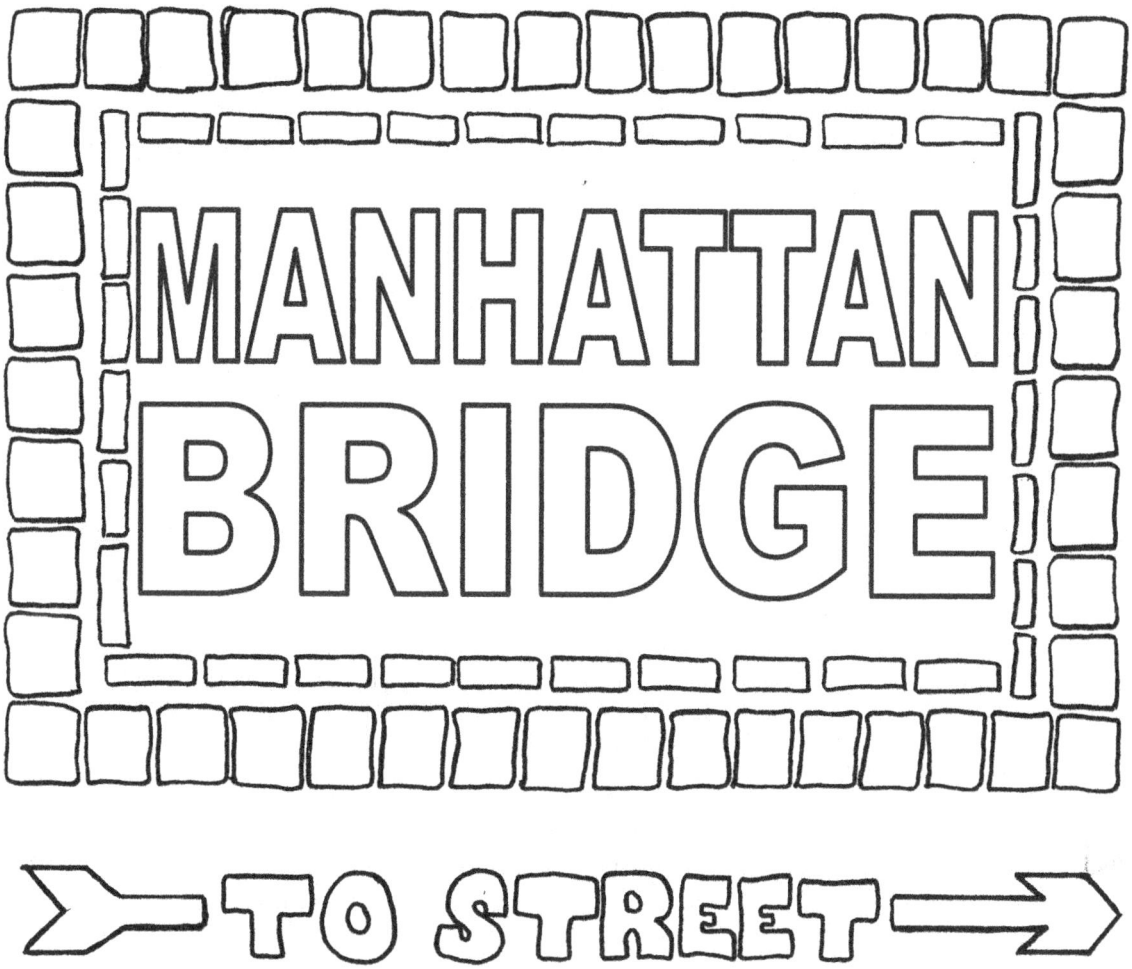
MANHATTAN
BRIDGE
TO STREET

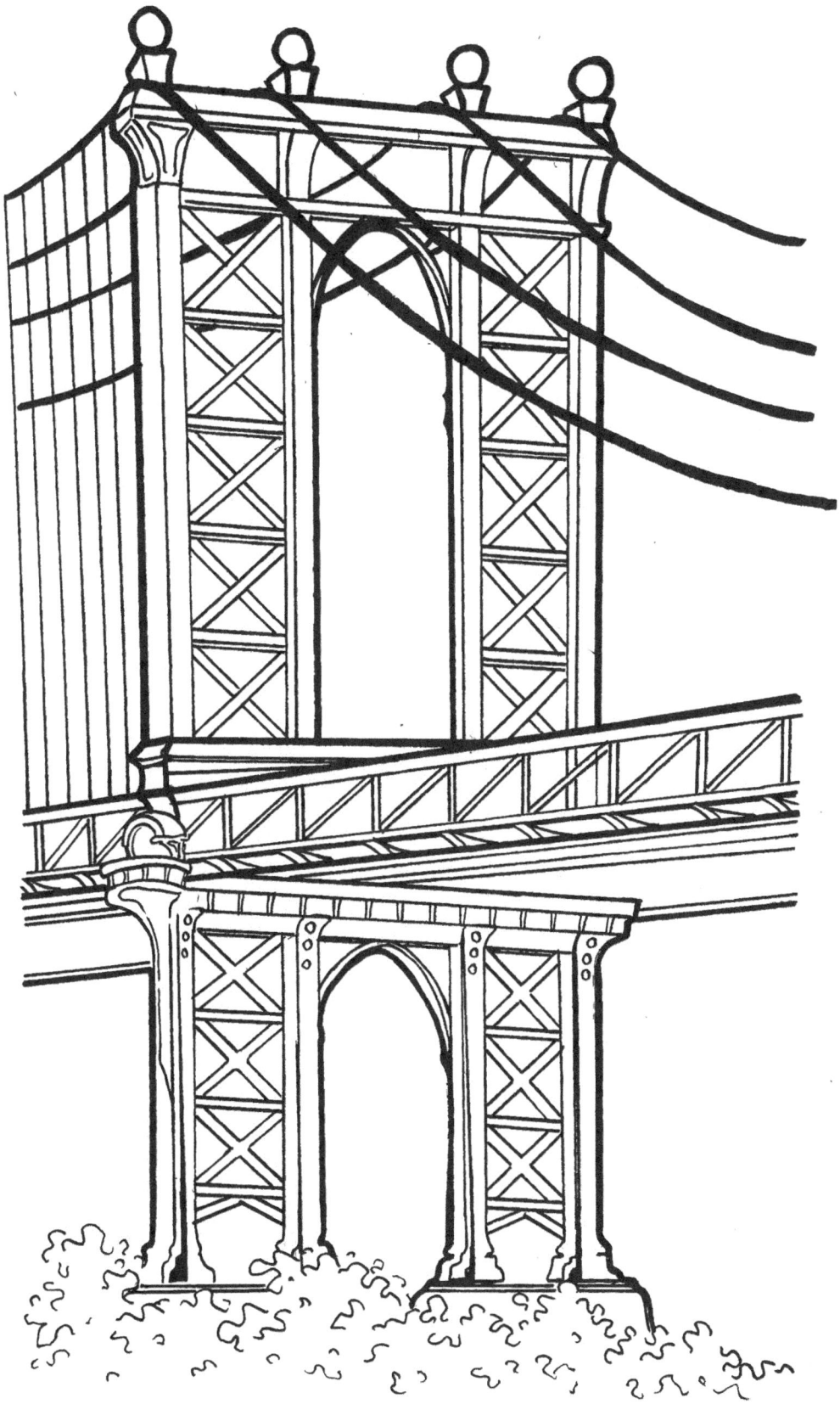

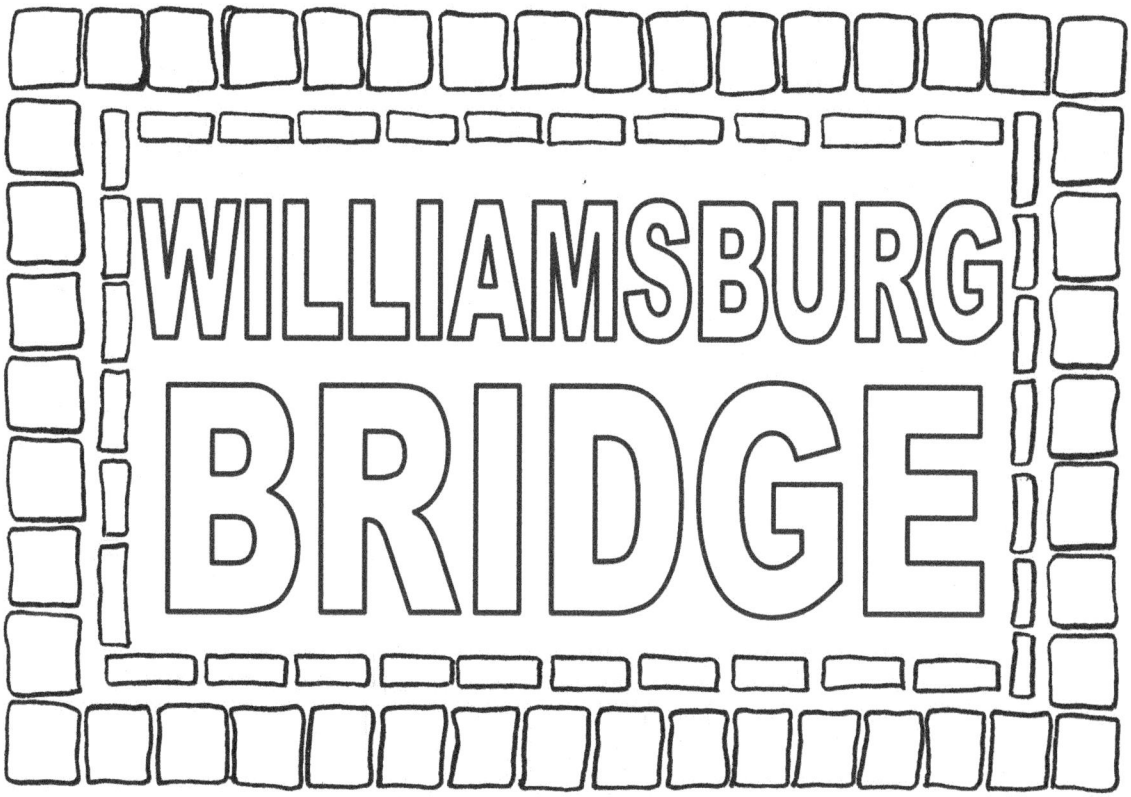
WILLIAMSBURG
BRIDGE

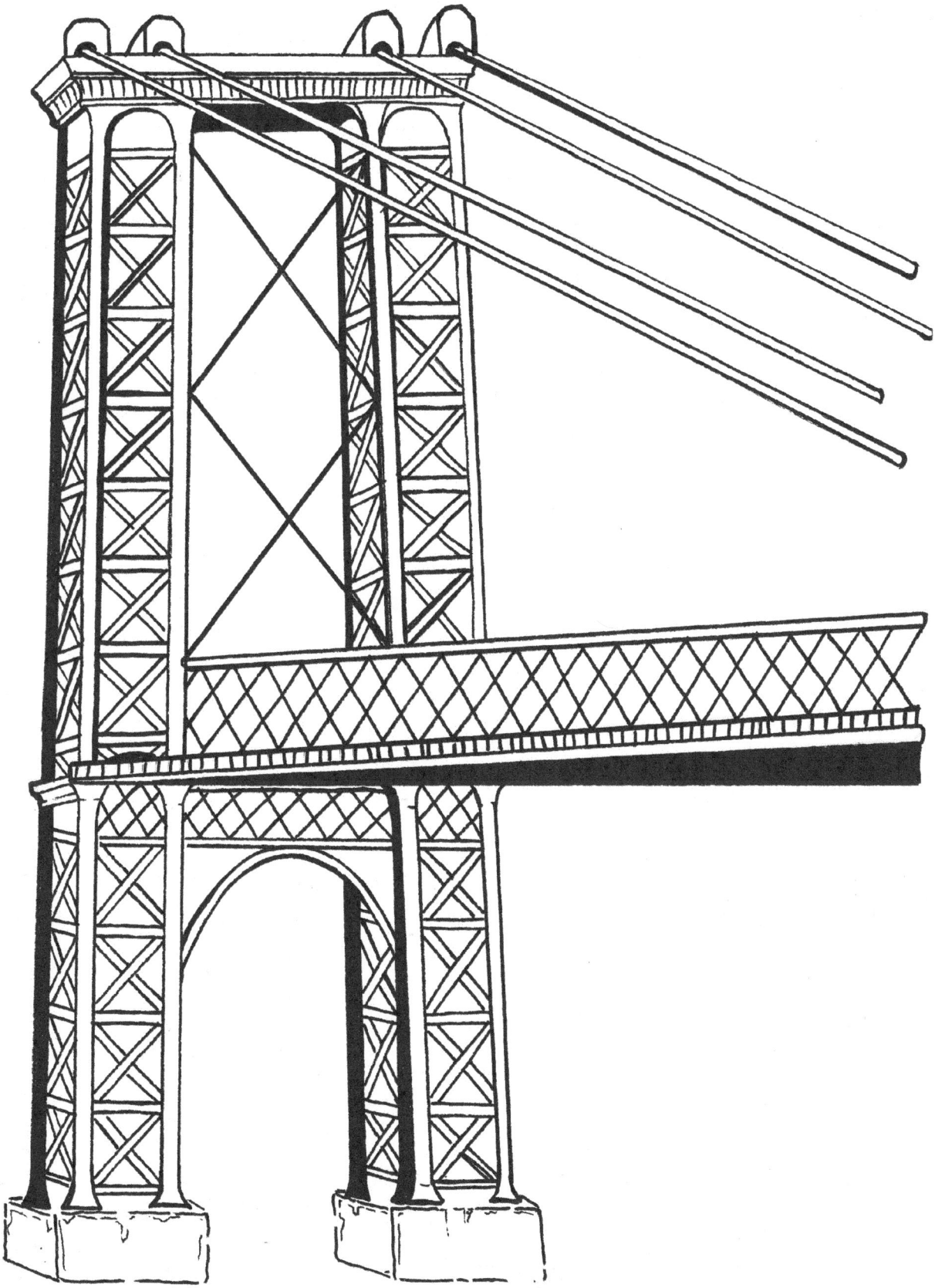

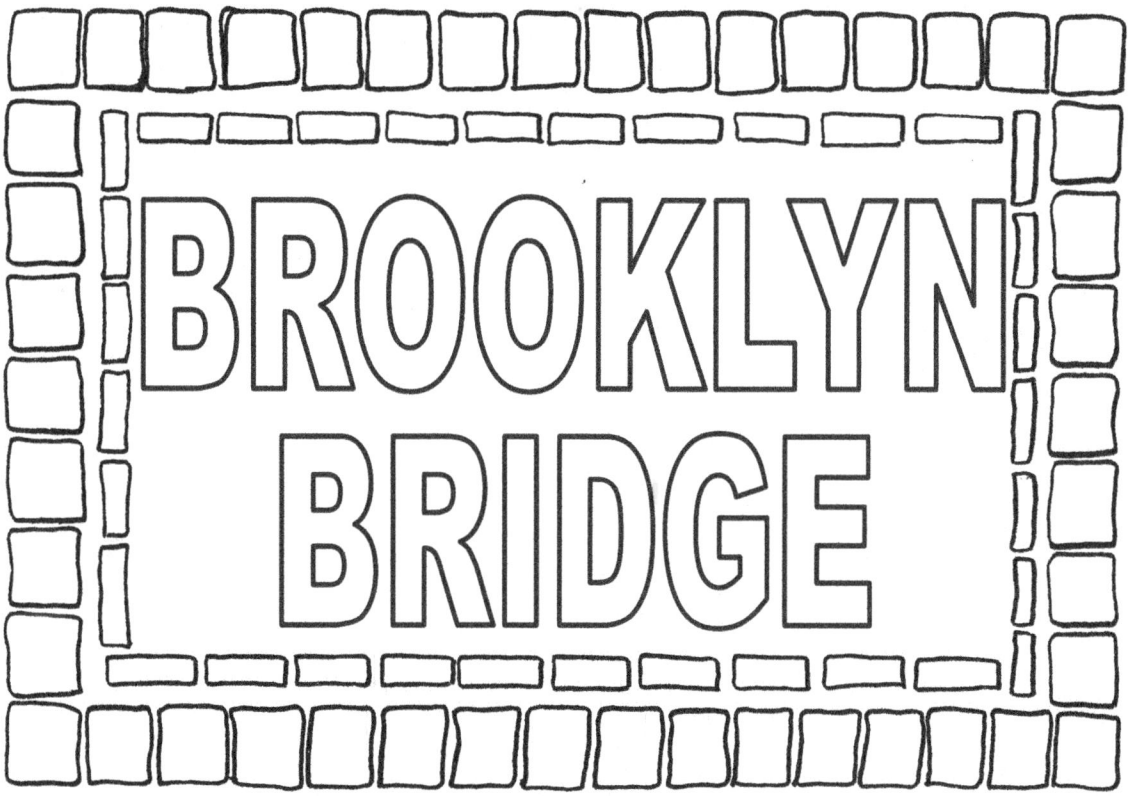
BROOKLYN
BRIDGE

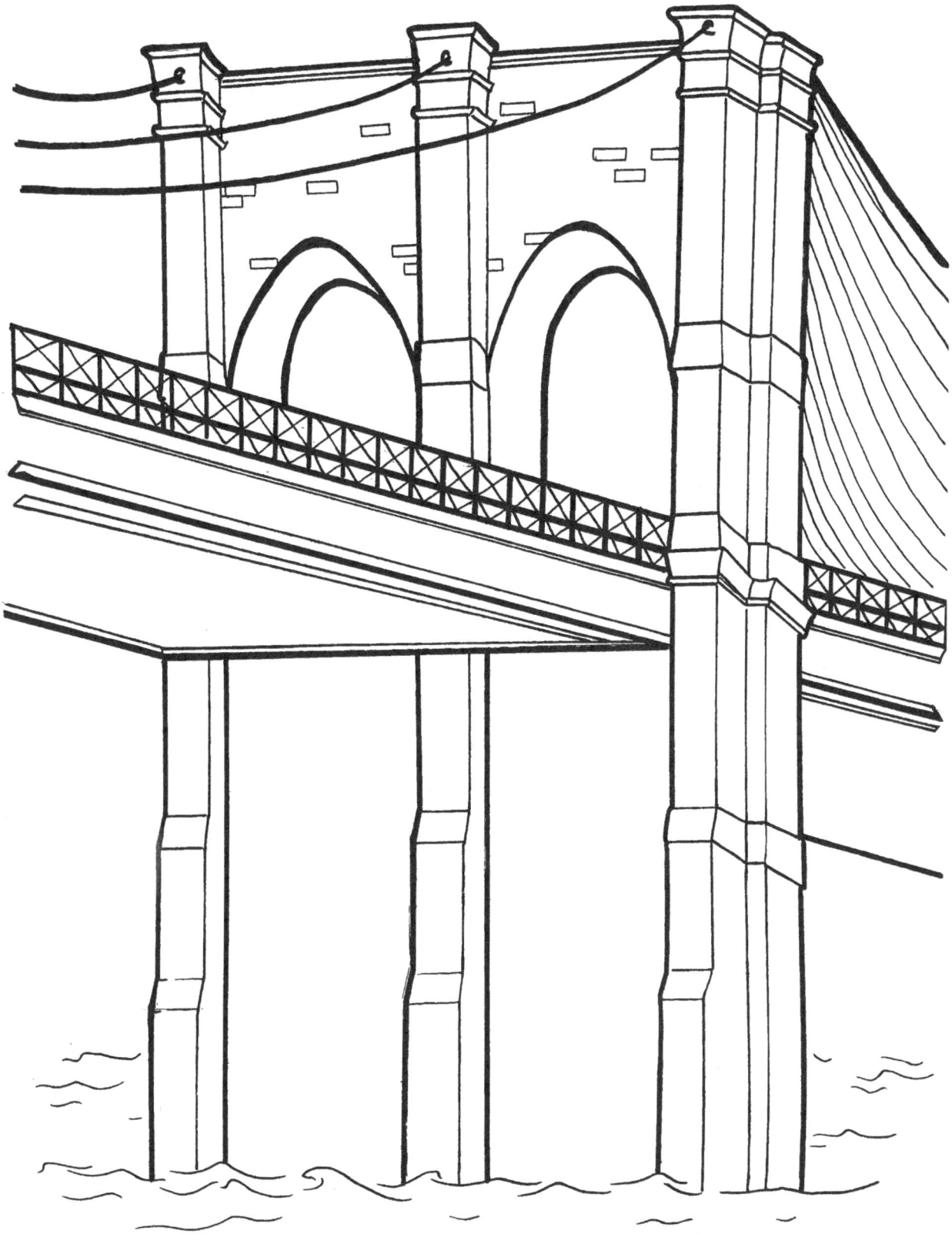

ABOUT THE ILLUSTRATOR

Mikayla Sherfy is an artist based in Brooklyn, New York. After moving from Missouri, where she was raised by a family of artists, Mikayla found inspiration in the beautifully complex NYC cityscape. She has been illustrating and painting it ever since, and her illustrations can be seen displayed in shops, offices, and galleries all around NYC. She never tires of exploring Brooklyn and has lived in many of the borough's neighborhoods, including the Navy Yard, Sunset Park, and Flatbush. Mikayla now lives and works in Greenpoint with her partner Adam and their dog Ferris. This is her first book.